The

inspiring
Grandmother

The

inspiring
Grandmother

90 Days of Devotions,
Prayer & Encouragement

DORIS RIKKERS and JEANNETTE TAYLOR,
general editors

Our Daily Bread
Publishing™

The Inspiring Grandmother:
90 Days of Devotions, Prayer & Encouragement
© 2008, 2017 by Jeannette Taylor and Doris Wynbeek Rikkers

Articles by Sheila Bailey, Michelle R. Loyd-Paige,
Victoria McAfee, Patricia Raybon, Diane Proctor Reeder,
and Kay Swatkowski © 2017 by Discovery House

Most articles first appeared in *The Grandmother's Bible*,
published by Zondervan. Used by permission.

Requests for permission to quote from this book should be directed to:
Permissions Department, Our Daily Bread Publishing, PO Box 3566, Grand
Rapids, MI 49501, or contact us by email at permissionsdept@odb.org.

Scripture quotations taken from the Holy Bible, New International Version®,
NIV®.Copyright © 1973, 1978, 1984, 2011 by Biblica, Inc.™ Used by
permissionof Zondervan. All rights reserved worldwide. zondervan.com.

Interior design by Beth Shagene

ISBN: 978-1-62707-872-6

Printed in the United States of America

20 21 22 23 24 25 26 / 8 7 6 5 4 3 2

Contents

Introduction

*Those who are wise will shine like the brightness
of the heavens, and those who lead many to
righteousness, like the stars for ever and ever.*
—DANIEL 12:3

Congratulations! If you're holding this book in your hands, you're probably a grandmother—one of the most wonderful callings in life. And as all of us already know, grandmothers are natural nurturers. Our grandchildren sense that. They run to us for love, a listening ear, a hug. As they grow older, they turn to us for sympathy and encouragement and advice. We have the wonderful opportunity to show God's love to our grandchildren by talking with them, spending time with them, praying for them, and sharing God's Word with them. Nurturing our grandchildren in a variety of ways is both a blessing and a calling from God.

But in order to continually nurture our grandchildren, we must also replenish our souls and nourish our own spiritual health. Along with studying God's Word, reading the devotions in this book will provide you with a daily boost of nourishment for your soul. Each devotion is written by grandmothers, for grandmothers, or about grandmothers with a specific focus that will help you grow in God's love and grace.

We pray that this devotional book will nourish your soul, will help you grow in spiritual wisdom, and will cause you to shine like the brightness of the heavens as you nurture your grandchildren and lead them in the way of righteousness.

Doris Rikkers
Jeannette Taylor
2017

day 1

The Invitation

*"Also I gave them my Sabbaths as a sign
between us, so they would know
that I the LORD made them holy."*
—EZEKIEL 20:12

When my granddaughter Abby was ten, she loved to hear stories at bedtime—and she didn't want fairy tales. She would say, "Tell me a true story, Nanny."

One night as Abby settled into bed, I rubbed her back and began: "Once there were two little girls who lived in the neighborhood where I grew up. I'm sad to tell you that the sisters grew up in a family that didn't go to church. A nice neighbor noticed the sisters wandering around or riding their bikes on Sunday mornings week after week. The neighbor thought the girls would enjoy making new friends, so she invited them to go to church with her family.

"Attending Sunday school and church became a weekly event for the little girls. Wearing their fancy dresses every Sunday, they enjoyed hugs, Bible stories, and beautiful music. They felt loved in the place where they could hear about Jesus. One Sunday *By Bobbie Wolgemuth* morning the girls invited Jesus to live in their hearts. They felt new and happier on the inside.

"That was a long time ago. The girls are grown up now, but they still go to church, and they sing the songs they learned when they were small."

Abby rolled over in bed to look at my face. "Why are you crying, Nanny?" she asked.

"Well, I'm really happy about the way the story turned out," I said with a smile. "You see, one of those little girls who long ago was invited to go to church by her neighbor—was me."

Leaving a legacy of faith may be as simple as telling your own story. Let your grandchild hear about the path that led you to Jesus.

We experience God's presence in a special way at church. You can encourage your grandchildren to find him there. Maybe there is someone you or your grandchild can invite to church this week.

A Prayer for You

Father in heaven, thank you for establishing the church as a stable, loving, serving family on earth. Help my children and grandchildren to overcome the challenges of their family's schedule and remember your gift of coming together as believers one day each week. Together with my family, I want to make it a wonderful day. Amen.

A Prayer for Your Grandchild
FOCUS: Worship

Dear Lord, you are worthy of worship. Please guide my grandchild to sense the value of worship, especially corporate worship with other believers in the body of Christ. Help him to know the value of meeting together at church with others who share a love for Jesus Christ, and help him to know that worshiping, learning from God's Word, and gaining insights from other believers at church are vital to his spiritual growth.

day 2

Cookies, Justice, and Mercy

He has shown you, O mortal, what is good.
*And what does the L*ORD *require of you?*
To act justly and to love mercy
and to walk humbly with your God.
—MICAH 6:8

Baking cookies at Grammy's house was always fun for five-year-old Morgan and three-year-old Jason. On the day I'm about to describe, they were diligently sharing assignments. While Morgan cracked the eggs, Jason sifted the flour. With a sudden "poof," flour was in the air and all over the floor!

"It's your fault, Jason!" Morgan cried indignantly as Jason looked helplessly at the mess on the floor. What just a moment before was pure pleasure was suddenly spoiled by angry accusations.

By Claudia Arp

Grammy, taking a deep breath, stepped in to help by kneeling beside the frozen little boy. "Jason, the cleanup sponge is under the sink. While you're wiping up, I'll get the dustpan."

When Morgan's accusations persisted, Grammy reminded her that she might need to collect herself on the little chair just around the corner. Jason whispered, "I'm sorry, Grammy. I made a mess."

"I'm sorry too, Jason," Grammy lovingly responded. "But sometimes accidents happen when I try new things. This is just a kitchen floor; we can clean it."

Frowning, Morgan watched from the corner of her eye as the cleanup proceeded. As Grammy and Jason got underway once again, her heart changed. Whirling around, she hugged Grammy. "I love you, Grammy! Jason, let's sift the flour again."

Our young grandchildren have a sweet innocence that affirms justice and mercy when they see it happening around them. If only we could have a pure heart like a child, we would deeply understand Micah 6:8. What does it mean to act justly, love mercy, and walk humbly with our God?

When we act justly, we live out what we believe through how we treat one another. When we love mercy, we are forgiving, compassionate, and tolerant. And as we walk humbly with God, we develop faithfulness. Then daily, with confidence and calmness, we can live out our commitment to each other and to God—even when we're making cookies with our grandkids.

A Prayer for You

Dear Lord and Father, please help me to live out justice, mercy, and a humble walk with you in all my relationships—especially with the precious grandchildren you have given to me. And help me to always remember that flour on the floor can easily be cleaned up.

A Prayer for Your Grandchild
FOCUS: Relationships at Home

O Lord, I pray that you will bless the home and family of my grandchild. May the relationships she has with her parents and siblings enhance her well-being, support her self-confidence, and increase her faith. May her home life reflect your love, your grace, your compassion, and your peace. Guide her parents to direct her in love and truth, so she will grow into a strong and compassionate individual. Amen.

day 3

Troubles: Big and Little

"They will pass through the sea of trouble;
the surging sea will be subdued . . .
I will strengthen them in the LORD
and in his name they will live securely,"
declares the LORD.
—ZECHARIAH 10:11–12

As a mother of ten, my maternal grandmother, Johanna Wynbeek, had many wise sayings about raising children. One family favorite was, "When they're little, the troubles are little; when they're big, the troubles are big."

Everyone who has raised children will acknowledge the wisdom in those words. We've been through the little troubles of infants and young children: ear infections, potty training, fear of monsters, separation anxiety. We know the midsize troubles of adolescents and teens: being picked on, body image, self-confidence, poor grades. We have suffered and agonized with our children as *By Doris Wynbeek Rikkers* they graduated from trouble to trouble. We've dropped everything when they've called, counseled them through sleepless nights, assisted and encouraged them in their decision-making. As our children move into adulthood, we expect them to handle their troubles on their own—yet because we love and care for them, we are never fully free.

No one is exempt from trouble; the Bible is clear on that. Jesus said, "In this world you will have trouble" (John 16:33). But the Bible also gives us good news about trouble. God has promised that although there will be trouble, we will "pass through" it (Zechariah 10:11); and He will be with us no matter what—nothing will separate us from His love (see Romans 8:35–39). Plus, God will strengthen us again when the trouble is past (Zechariah 10:12).

My grandmother was not exempt from trouble. To name just a few of her challenges in life: her firstborn daughter died as an infant; another daughter suffered illness and seizures; her husband died at age forty-eight, leaving her alone to raise her children. Through all her troubles Johanna's faith remained constant. Although it was difficult, she knew that the Lord would provide and that He would give her strength to face whatever troubles life presented. He was there for Johanna; He is there for us too.

A Prayer for You

Dear Lord, thank you for your presence in all the troubles I face in life. Thank you for the promise that trouble will pass and that you will strengthen me to continue my walk with you. Amen.

A Prayer for Your Grandchild
FOCUS: Courage

O Father, builder of character and courage, may my grandchild grow strong in the light of your face. Grant him courage to stand for what is right, to guard the truth, and to ensure justice in every aspect of life. May he boldly grow in grace, revere your name, and proudly proclaim you as the Lord of Lords and King of Kings.

day 4

From Womb to World

For you have been my hope, Sovereign LORD,
my confidence since my youth.
From birth I have relied on you;
you brought me forth from my mother's womb.
I will ever praise you.
—PSALM 71:5–6

It's comforting to look back and see God's hand in my life. In so many ways he has indeed been "my confidence since my youth," as Psalm 71:5 describes. Through the occasional nightmare in childhood; through the forking roads of middle school, when choices had to be made; then in high school, where those choices became values to be held; and eventually on into early adulthood and fresh, eager marriage, where so much "self" was revealed and redirected. Indeed, God has been my confidence since youth.

While my own children came to me from the womb of another—they were both adopted—I keenly felt God's presence in their safe delivery into my arms. Today, while I'm in the season of grandbabies, Psalm 71:6 comforts me with God's presence even in the *By Elisa Morgan* manner in which a child comes into a family. "From birth I have relied on you; you brought me forth from my mother's womb."

As we hold our grandbabies in our arms, we see the journey of life yawning before them with its crossroads, bends, and turns. With the perspective fashioned out of

20

living life fully ourselves, we tense in expectation at both the joy and the tragedy surely ahead. Knowing for them what we could not know for ourselves, we trust that God's presence, so precious in our youth, will be the same abiding presence in their days.

A Prayer for You

Dear God, as you have brought little ones into your world, may they rely on you today and in all the days ahead. Just as you oversaw the birth of each child, may you oversee the steps and the choices ahead, and may each child welcome your presence as you guide him or her. Amen.

A Prayer for Your Grandchild
FOCUS: Spiritual Growth

Dear Lord, today I pray for my grandchild's spiritual growth. I ask that you instill in him the desire to read and memorize your Word. Give him a passion to be in conversation with you. May loving and serving you be part of his daily life. I ask that you stay close to him and lead him to be transformed to your likeness, to reflect your grace, and to radiate your love. I pray this in Jesus's name, amen.

day 5

No Longer Outcasts

There is neither Jew nor Gentile,
neither slave nor free,
nor is there male and female,
for you are all one in Christ Jesus.
—GALATIANS 3:28

I grew up in the segregated South in the 1940s and 1950s, when there was designated seating for "Colored" and "White" people in street cars, theaters, and schools—as well as water fountains marked for each race. Fascinated by the designations and always curious about the difference in those signs, I bravely determined, by disobeying the signs, that the only difference between the "Colored" water and the "White" water was the temperature. The "Colored" was hot; the "White" was cold.

My granddaddy often took me to the Majestic Theatre, where we had to sit in the balcony (called the "buzzard roost") and eat the stale candy and popcorn. I'll always remember his prediction: "Pooch *By Thelma Wells* (that's what he affectionately called me), one of these days you're gonna be able to walk in this theater through the front door and sit in the front row or box seats. You watch and see."

It's true. I've been through the front door and strolled down to the front row, center aisle, of that very theater. In God's time, he makes all things beautiful—no matter how ugly they may seem.

You might feel discriminated against or like an outcast in one way or the other. Jesus did. He wasn't welcome in His own hometown. He knows how you feel. He never discriminates against you—no matter who you are. He loves you and wants the best for you.

When you feel like an outcast, remember that Jesus calls you His child. You're safe with Him, just like I was safe with my granddaddy. Jesus has opened the door for you to walk in and have a front-row seat in His presence. You are always welcome!

A Prayer for You

Kind Father, thank you for making all believers one in Christ Jesus. Thank you that there are no barriers between us and that all of your children are always welcome in your presence. Help me to treat others the way you treat me. In Jesus's name, amen.

A Prayer for Your Grandchild
FOCUS: Overcoming Prejudice

She's so young, O Lord, to be judged by how she looks. So grow my precious grandchild by her character. Strengthen her heart and mind, her soul and spirit— filling her with the knowledge, depth, goodness, and joy of you. Help her to know that her heart, not her appearance, defines who she is. More than all, help her to see, believe, and know this: You are the Christ! Amen.

day 6

The Missing Glasses

"Are not two sparrows sold for a penny?
Yet not one of them will fall to the ground outside
your Father's care. And even the very hairs
of your head are all numbered. So don't be afraid;
you are worth more than many sparrows."
—MATTHEW 10:29–31

God is a personal God, and He is interested in the details of our lives. Jesus said the very hairs on our head are numbered! My grandson Wyatt and I have personally experienced God's caring for life's little details.

Some years ago we discovered that my grandson was very farsighted. He hated his thick-lens prescription glasses, so he was a bit careless in how he treated them—much to his mom's frustration.

One evening my phone rang. Wyatt was on the other end, but I could not understand what he was trying to tell me between his sobs. Finally, he was able to tell me that he had lost his glasses and his mom had

By Ruth Graham

lost patience with him—demanding he locate his glasses NOW (they were new and expensive).

His distress was palpable over the phone. I asked the typical questions: "Where did you last have them?" "Do you remember taking them off?" He either couldn't remember or assured me that he had looked everywhere.

Finally, with desperation and diminishing hope, I said, "Wyatt, let's ask Jesus to help you find your glasses."

We prayed together over the phone and asked Jesus to help Wyatt find the glasses. Wyatt hung up with a sigh. As I put the receiver down, my faith wavered. Had I set Wyatt up for disappointment? I quietly asked God to answer in a way that would build Wyatt's faith—and my own. "I do believe; help me overcome my unbelief!" (see Mark 9:24).

A short time later, Wyatt called back with a much happier tone in his voice. He had found his glasses on the bookshelf next to his bed! We prayed again, thanking God for answering our prayer and asking God to build our faith. I then thanked Him for caring about the details of not only my grandson's life but my life as well.

A Prayer for You

O God, increase my faith. May I never doubt your Word and your promise that you care about the smallest details in my life. Let me confidently come to you and place my every concern at your feet. Amen.

A Prayer for Your Grandchild
FOCUS: Relationships at Home

O Lord, I pray that you will bless the home and family of my grandchild. May the relationships he has with his parents and siblings enhance his well-being, support his self-confidence, and increase his faith. May his home life reflect your love, your grace, your compassion, and your peace. Guide his parents to direct him in love and truth so he will grow into a strong and compassionate individual. Amen.

day 7

Made in God's Image

God created mankind in his own image,
in the image of God he created them;
male and female he created them.
—GENESIS 1:27

I was a very young grandmother. This was not all that surprising since I had been a young bride and a young mother. But when Randy, our firstborn son, married and gave us our first grandchild, I was completely unprepared.

I was especially unprepared for the love I would feel for this baby. I was amazed that the love I had felt so strongly for my sons—a love I was positive would never be duplicated—tripled when my first grandson's newborn eyes slowly opened to meet mine. Oh, those eyes! So trusting and innocent! I gave my heart so completely, so swiftly to this new little one named James that the bonding left me breathless.

When I left the hospital after seeing James for the first time, I was filled with joy—with songs of joy. As I enjoyed my ecstatic state, I recalled the words of the psalmist, "Our mouths were filled with laughter, our tongues with songs of joy" (Psalm 126:2). Little did I know that this child was not only a precious gift to me (though he was) but he was also God's special gift to the world. God in His miraculous grace was enlarging His

By Lori Copeland

kingdom through this tiny scrap of humanity created in His image (see Genesis 1:27).

James is a grown man now, a husband, a father, and a pastor. He has many times ministered to the Kagoro tribe in Africa and, through God's unending grace, led lost souls to Christ. As a thirty-nine-year-old grandmother, I had no idea what God had placed in my life the day my first grandson was born. But now, many years later, I stand astounded at His marvelous workings.

A Prayer for You

Thank you, God, for placing grandchildren in my life and into my care as a grandmother. As they grow, lead them in the ways of righteousness, that their days may be long and fruitful on this earth. Amen.

A Prayer for Your Grandchild
FOCUS: Self-Image

O loving God, I praise you for creating my grandchild as a special, unique individual. Now I ask you to help her appreciate her uniqueness. Build up her self-image so she can enjoy her individuality. Help her to stand for who she is, where she has come from, and what she believes in. Encourage her not only to have hopes and dreams for the future but also to enjoy each day as it comes. In Jesus's name, amen.

day 8

Give Them Corn

"When anyone hears the message about the kingdom and does not understand it, the evil one comes and snatches away what was sown in their heart."
—MATTHEW 13:19

My four grandchildren had come to Sanibel Island, Florida, to vacation with me. That meant golden days of sunshine, shelling, and sandcastles. One morning while they all still slept, I sat on the porch with my mug of coffee, watching the ocean turn crimson as the sun crept over the horizon. I thought of how God had assured Job that He was, indeed, in control of life (see Job 38:1–15).

By Dee Brestin

At that moment nine-year-old Simeon appeared, rubbing sleep from his eyes. I knew what he was going to ask before he even spoke. The hotel had a video arcade that had been drawing little boys like magnets.

"Grandma, can I please have a dollar for the video arcade?"

"Come here, honey. Climb on Grandma's lap."

He climbed up and snuggled for about ten seconds before asking again, "Can I have a dollar, please?"

"Memorize the first three verses of Job 38 and you may."

He hopped down, running for a Bible. In five minutes he was back, reciting the verses perfectly.

"Wonderful, Simeon! Now tell me why God said that to Job."

"You didn't tell me I had to know what it meant!" My grandson and I exchanged smiles. He knew me well enough to know there would be no dollar until he had captured the meaning. Charles Spurgeon said that if we give children stories without being sure they understand the meaning, it is like giving them the husk of the corn without the golden kernels.

Simeon climbed back on my lap, and we had a ten-minute discussion. When we were done, I asked again, "Why did God say that to Job?"

"Sometimes God asks us questions to help us trust Him." I nodded.

"YES!" Simeon exclaimed, hopping down to get me my purse.

A Prayer for You

Father, as I tell my grandchildren your amazing stories, help me to help them understand the meaning behind them. May the meaning penetrate deep into their hearts so the evil one cannot snatch it away.

A Prayer for Your Grandchild
FOCUS: Protection from Worldliness

O Sovereign Lord, the world surrounds my grandchild, pressing in and tempting him in so many ways. Help him set appropriate limits. Give him sound judgment to choose wisely. Guard him from temptation, protect him from physical and mental predators, and lead him into paths of righteousness and light. And reassure me with your promise that you are holding him in your hands. In Jesus's name, amen.

day 9

The Right Words

*Do not let any unwholesome talk come out
of your mouths, but only what is helpful
for building others up according to their needs,
that it may benefit those who listen.*
—EPHESIANS 4:29

Four-year-old PJ and I were food shopping together, and he wasn't a very happy boy.

"Grandmom, can I have those cookies?"

"I don't think so, honey."

"Then I want a candy bar."

"Not today."

"Ice cream. You can get me ice cream."

"No ice cream. I told you that you could get one thing—which is more than I used to tell your daddy—and you already picked it out. That's it, sweetheart."

He looked at me with great dislike, folded his arms over his chest and said, "I'm going to get my mommy to beat you up."

I didn't laugh in his face, but it was a struggle to keep a straight face. He looked so disgruntled—a little eaglet with all his feathers ruffled, a strong-willed child resentful about not getting his own way.

By Gayle Roper

When a little guy says something so outrageous, it's funny, but how many times do we supposedly mature adults say things just as ridiculous? "Do that again, and you're grounded

30

for life!" "I don't care if spinach makes you throw up. Eat it."

Even worse, how often do we say things that are hurtful? "You are such a dunce!" "Man, am I glad you're not my kid. At least I can send you home to your parents."

That old platitude about sticks and stones breaking our bones but words never hurting is *so* untrue. Words can wound. Words can even kill the spirit. Instead, we can choose words that build up. We can see that our speech is seasoned with grace. We can make our grandkids feel they're the most important people in the world—at least our world—with the right words.

A Prayer for You

Father, help me speak words that are wholesome and that build up my grandchildren and all the others in my life. May I think before I speak. For the glory of your name. Amen.

A Prayer for Your Grandchild
FOCUS: Spiritual Growth

Dear Lord, today I pray for my grandchild's spiritual growth. I ask that you instill in her the desire to read and memorize your Word. Give her a passion to be in conversation with you. May loving and serving you be part of her daily life. I ask that you stay close to her and lead her to be transformed to your likeness, to reflect your grace, and to radiate your love. I pray this in Jesus's name, amen.

day **10**

The Refrigerator Door

*Joshua set up at Gilgal the twelve stones
they had taken out of the Jordan.*
—JOSHUA 4:20

When our children were growing up, our refrigerator door looked like a wonderful, messy collage of scribbled artwork, photographs, various school schedules, cartoons, quotes, Scripture verses, and personal messages. Then in our early empty-nest years, we totally cleared off the clutter. Our refrigerator door looked refreshingly clean—and boring.

Thankfully, our refrigerator door has taken on a meaningful personality once again. Along with photographs of our grandchildren, we have brightly crayoned pieces of priceless art—mostly of stick-figure families and pointy-edged suns. I love our refrigerator door once again because it is filled with visual aids *By Carol Kuykendall* that remind us of the importance of our grandchildren in our lives. I hope these visual aids give our grandchildren the same message.

I believe that God created us as visual learners who respond well to visual aids. The Bible contains many examples, such as the monument of twelve stones piled up at Gilgal to remind the people of God's great faithfulness in miraculously enabling them to cross the Jordan River at flood stage (Joshua 4:20). Visual aids are powerful reminders of an important message.

Children depend on outside sources to meet their need for love, which gives them a foundation of security and confidence. That was true for my own children, and it is also true for my grandchildren. When they come into our house and see their artwork and photos on our refrigerator and scattered throughout our house, I hope they are reminded that they are loved and that they matter greatly to us.

That's an important message.

A Prayer for You

Lord, you teach us that visual aids are powerful reminders. May we use them to remind our grandchildren of your love for us and our love for them.

A Prayer for Your Grandchild
FOCUS: Self-Image

O loving God, I praise you for creating my grandchild as a special, unique individual. Now I ask you to help him appreciate his uniqueness. Build up his self-image so he can enjoy his individuality. Help him to stand for who he is, where he has come from, and what he believes in. Encourage him not only to have hopes and dreams for the future but also to enjoy each day as it comes. In Jesus's name, amen.

day 11

Generations of Faith

"I will establish my covenant as an everlasting covenant between me and you and your descendants after you for the generations to come, to be your God and the God of your descendants after you."
—GENESIS 17:7

I never met my grandmother on my mom's side of the family. Doris Parsons died at age forty-five, a young victim of breast cancer. She left behind five kids; her youngest was only eight years old at the time. My mom was the oldest, just twenty-two and newly married to my father. So my mom is the one who has filled me in on the details of my grandma's life.

Doris was a dynamic woman, a woman with a passion for God, for family, and for something very dear to my heart: books. You see, Doris was a librarian, and it is in that one detail that I see Genesis 17:7 come to life. God made promises to His people, a covenant that would last for generations to come. That covenant involved life—ultimately eternal life through our Savior Jesus Christ. But it was also a covenant of connectivity, a covenant of faith.

By Karen Kingsbury

A few years ago, my mom and I took a trip to Canada to visit the grave where Grandma Doris is buried. Since she died just three months before I was born, I wanted to feel that connectivity, to know that I was standing in the same spot where my grandfather once stood, grieving the loss of his vibrant wife.

Sometimes I can picture Grandma Doris smiling down from heaven, seeing the covenant of faith passed on from her to my mom and then passed down again to me. How thrilled she would have been to know that her granddaughter became an author and that, through those books, God would use the power of story to change lives for His kingdom. How gracious our God is to demonstrate the strength of connection through generations of faith.

A Prayer for You

Dear Lord, I pray that I would see great value in the lives of those who lived before me, in the connectivity of generations, and in the lessons of faith learned. Let me also be a shining example of your grace and power to my children and grandchildren. In Christ's name, amen.

A Prayer for Your Grandchild
FOCUS: Future Spouse

Dear Lord, if it is your will, I pray my grandchild will be united in a loving and Christian marriage. Keep him sexually pure so he will honor you with his body and mind. As he seeks a spouse who will honor and care for him, give him patience and discernment. May his choice for a life partner be your choice for him, so he and his wife will together glorify you in a lasting love. I pray this in Jesus's name, amen.

day 12

"You're Doing Beautifully"

Like apples of gold in settings of silver
is a ruling rightly given.
—PROVERBS 25:11

Three daughters. Pink frills, dolls, jump rope, dress up, music, drama. What fun we had together as they grew up! Of course, there were sibling rivalries, hormones, and many tears. There were discipline challenges that sent a weary mother to her knees in dependence upon God, praying for wisdom and strength.

Three college degrees. Three weddings. Eight grandchildren! My daughters are good mothers and loving wives. Each is uniquely creative and talented. Each is different from me and has her own

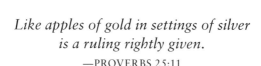

By Rebecca Lutzer

way of running her home and disciplining her children. I have had to accept that my daughters do not want or need my advice about some things. Indeed, I have learned some painful lessons in this area.

However, they do need my love, encouragement, respect, affirmation, and prayers—without criticism and judgment. "Like apples of gold in settings of silver is a ruling rightly given" (Proverbs 25:11). When I disagree, I must speak in love and with carefully chosen words. I must respect their autonomy and pray over matters that concern me.

My daughters are experiencing the same joys and

challenges I did, plus ones I didn't: husbands deployed to Afghanistan for twelve months or laid off for seven months or taking a new job in another state; children stillborn or hospitalized or traumatized by a father's long absence.

Whether a large or small trial, I tell my daughters that God is always faithful to His Word. He loves them. His grace is sufficient.

"Trust Him." "Obey Him." "Don't give up." "Keep going." "I'm praying for you."

Often, these words are just what they need: "You're doing beautifully, and you will make it, just like I did!"

A Prayer for You

Dear loving heavenly Father, thank you for the precious gift of children. Please sustain, comfort, and teach them by the Holy Spirit's power. Please give them grace, wisdom, and patience to meet each day and each trial, so they may become godly women and men. Give me discernment and gracious words to uphold and encourage them. Amen.

A Prayer for Your Grandchild
FOCUS: Spiritual Growth

Dear Lord, today I pray for my grandchild's spiritual growth. I ask that you instill in him the desire to read and memorize your Word. Give him a passion to be in conversation with you. May loving and serving you be part of his daily life. I ask that you stay close to him and lead him to be transformed to your likeness, to reflect your grace, and to radiate your love. I pray this in Jesus's name, amen.

day 13

Cutting the Apron Strings . . . for Real

All these are the twelve tribes of Israel, and this is what their father said to them when he blessed them, giving each the blessing appropriate to him.
—GENESIS 49:28

One of the wisest women I ever met was an unassuming secretary. I don't remember her name, but I'll never forget the lesson she taught me. I was a young mother in the throes of seeing my children grow into young adults, and I was all ears for advice that could make that transition easier.

Somehow, in our brief woman-to-woman conversation, the question came up about how she let her children go. She quietly smiled and said, "I gave them apron strings." She continued with her explanation. "I raised my children alone. Their father was gone, and as each child grew, I knew there would be a time when they would have to become responsible for themselves. I wanted them to view that step as an honor, a rite of passage, not just something they had to do because I had limited resources and they didn't have a daddy to help them launch."

By Jan Silvious

"So when my first child turned eighteen, I cut the strings off my apron, wrapped them in a box with a beautiful bow, and wrote her a note declaring that 'the apron strings were now officially cut.' I told her I admired who she had become and would support her in prayer as she found her way into adulthood. There were other small gifts that day, but the box of apron strings was her most treasured one. She was thrilled with the newfound respect and status that little ceremony gave her. I repeated that celebration four more times, until my nest was empty. All five of my children cherished the apron strings, and I believe the affirmation that gave them as they became young adults was critical to who they eventually became."

A Prayer for You

Father, give me the grace to approve my grown children with affirming words and meaningful blessings. Help me to remember that what I say (or don't say) will be with them always. Amen.

A Prayer for Your Grandchild
FOCUS: Emotional Development

O God, Creator of mind and body, I pray that you will give my grandchild emotional health and strength. Where there is anger, bring peace. Where there is confusion, bring clarity and focus. Where there are dark shadows, cast a ray of hope. Fill her with the sunshine of your Spirit. Warm her with the presence of your peace. In Jesus's name, amen.

day 14

Loving Despite the Differences

"God does not show favoritism."
—ACTS 10:34

They look white. I am black. Such is my story with our three precious youngest grandchildren. They were born in our family's interracial, interfaith, "Heinz 57" clan—formed when our younger daughter turned from the cross, converted to Islam, and married a young man whose dad is German American and whose mother is Mexican American. "Heinz 57" and more, indeed.

Things got more complicated, however, when our light-skinned black daughter and her biracial husband birthed my three sweet little grandchildren. Who look white. So when we are all together, we

By Patricia Raybon

get stares. In grocery stores. At shopping malls. In their schools. I know what the looks mean: *You, an African-American woman, are the grandmother of these children?*

Well, yes, I am. Yet the questioning and judgmental looks bothered me for a long time.

I felt self-conscious and accused, as if I needed to explain, even to strangers, why our family doesn't look as if we necessarily belong together.

I've known that tension for a long time, however. Some thirty years ago, when my daughter was a toddler and I pushed her through a grocery store in a shopping cart, a woman actually stopped me in a food aisle, pointing at my light-skinned Alana: "Is she *your* baby? Was she in your basket the last aisle I passed you?"

Her question taunted me, as if I'd stolen my own child. Shocked by the woman's accusation, I knew I needed a solution—not for others, for myself. The Lord graciously provided it. *Love all your children.* As Jesus loves.

Despite their color or creed. Hug, play, listen, laugh, sing, teach, and love them. Like Jesus. With no favorites. In return, they love me back. Then seeing love, people surely know. We are family.

A Prayer for You

O God of all, you loved me when I was broken and close-hearted. Empower me now by your Holy Spirit to love as lavishly as you, regardless of creed or color, especially in my complex family. Then by my bold love, may each of my grandchildren see your welcoming heart. Amen.

A Prayer for Your Grandchild
FOCUS: Overcoming Prejudice

He's so young, O Lord, to be judged by how he looks. So grow my precious grandchild by his character. Strengthen his heart and mind, his soul and spirit— filling him with the knowledge, depth, goodness and joy of you. Help him to know that his heart, not his appearance, defines who he is. More than all, help him to see, believe, and know: You are the Christ. Amen.

day 15

Liam's Smelling Game

Therefore, as God's chosen people, holy and
dearly loved, clothe yourselves with compassion,
kindness, humility, gentleness and patience.
—COLOSSIANS 3:12

Four-year-old Liam scurried up the front porch steps. "It's me, Grandpa!" he announced to my husband, who was sitting in a wooden Adirondack chair, both eyes bandaged after eye surgery. "Daddy and I brought you a game to play!"

It wasn't the first time Liam had shown concern for the ordeal his grandpa was going through. It started out with one eye operation, which kept my husband facedown for three weeks. Liam made a paper chain

By Neta Jackson

out of construction paper, so Grandpa could tear one off for each day that passed. The phone rang every few days, and a childish voice would ask, "How are your eyes doing today, Grandpa?"

Then things began to go wrong. Another operation . . . another procedure . . . and another . . . until my husband's eye was so traumatized the doctors didn't dare try another. So they bandaged both eyes and told him to "keep still; don't move."

Not being able to see at all was the greatest test of all.

But now our son and grandson showed up, ready to play. "A game?" asked my husband, as he reached for the little boy and pulled him into a hug. "But I can't see right now."

"That's okay, Grandpa. It's a smelling game. And I'm going to play it with you."

He instructed his daddy to blindfold him, "just like Grandpa." Then the game was brought out: a tray of little tins with smelly items in them—garlic, a flower, vinegar, horseradish, etc.—and Grandpa with his eye patches and grandson with his blindfold tried to guess each smell.

As I watched Liam putting himself in his grandpa's place and trying to cheer him up, my own eyes got teary. I had just read Colossians 3 and realized I was seeing a truly "best-dressed" child (v. 12).

A Prayer for You

O God, let me be more concerned with being "clothed" with compassion and kindness than worrying about how my hair looks or whether my outfit is too dated. Children don't care what they're wearing; they just want to love and be loved.

A Prayer for Your Grandchild
FOCUS: School/Career

Dear God, may learning be a joy rather than a chore for my grandchild. May exploration of new ideas bring a sense of wonder, awe, and excitement. Grant him clarity of mind, the ability to concentrate on the task at hand, and recollection of what has been learned. Help him to appreciate the tasks that come easily and to persevere through those that challenge. Amen.

day **16**

Memories and Bridges

Children are a heritage from the LORD,
offspring a reward from him.
—PSALM 127:3

I had lost two grandmothers and one great grandmother by the time I was six. My father's mother passed when I was three; I was so tiny I only remember her from the waist down. My mother's grandmother passed when I was that same age, and I only remember her lumbering down the steps at my grandparents' house. She was short and stout. I did not know either of them well enough to grieve.

My mother's mother died suddenly and tragically when she unwittingly mixed blood pressure medication with a powerful weight loss supplement. The year was 1964, and I was six years old. I still remember the pungent smell of her cologne as she picked me up and hugged me when I came over.

Years later, my mother would bequeath me another memory when she handed me a small black three-ringed binder that held my grandmother's hand-written notes listing the titles of every book she read by year in the 1930s; and a surfeit of sublime poetry and prayers, again written

By Diane Proctor Reeder

in her perfect penmanship. The poems detailed her love for God and her family.

And now I'm a grandmother. My precious granddaughter Gabbi, at the tender age of four, has seven grandparents and great-grandparents—an abundance of riches that I envy. I am grateful that she will have the benefit of that godly wisdom and an abundance of love that only grandparents understand.

It is our memories that make up who we are. And it occurs to me that the richness of the generations that go before us makes us all the more rich in the things that matter: faith, hope, and love. This is the idea of heritage we read about in theory in Psalm 127 and in reality in 2 Timothy 1.

When I keep Gabbi at night, she likes to lie close to me . . . sometimes she asks me to lie on my back so she can straddle on top of my stomach. I feel her beating heart and her soft breath on my neck, and I pray. I hope she remembers my beating heart and the love that emanates. And I hope she will use those visceral memories as scaffolding for the bridge that carries her over to her own faith-journeys.

A Prayer for You

Lord, help me to give to my grandchildren the memory of holiness, without which no one can see God; the memory of the Light that lights all who come into the world; and the memory of laughter, which is better than medicine.

A Prayer for Your Grandchild
FOCUS: Heritage

Lord, make my grandchild a sacred bridge between our generations. Help him to reach back and see the faith of his ancestors who have gone before. Help him to treat as sacred the road he is laying down for his own children to travel. Give him eyes that see forward as they look backward. Put eternity in his heart.

day 17

A Tale of Two Angels

*"Therefore I tell you, whatever you ask
for in prayer, believe that you have received it,
and it will be yours."*
—MARK 11:24

Our son, a recent graduate of the US Naval Academy, called with unexpected news: "My orders have changed. I have to be at Surface Warfare Officers' School in Newport, Rhode Island, on September 8. April and I are in love, and we want to get married next Friday."

I was stunned. My son was asking to marry a woman I had never met, a previously married woman with two children—*next Friday*. Rational thinking slowly returned. We asked Jason and his fiancée if they would wait three weeks and be married in our hometown. They agreed.

Jason and April walked through our front door with arms encircling each other's waists. April had been married at the age of sixteen to a man ten years her senior, and she had been through more of the "tough stuff of life" than *By Carol Kent* anyone deserves. Behind them were six-year-old Chelsea and three-year-old Hannah. Minutes later Chelsea took my hand in her two hands, looked up and said, "You're my new favorite Grammy!"

Every morning Hannah ate her cereal, singing between bites, "I love Jesus; He loves me!" The girls invaded my closet and dressed up in chiffon and long beads. They won my heart very quickly.

As the wedding day approached, I saw deep love in the eyes of my son and his bride. And I already loved my big, brown-eyed granddaughters. I wasn't there for their births, but they were filling my heart with so much joy. Two little angels entered my life at an unexpected time and showered me with unconditional love and acceptance. I had a new name: Grammy! And I had a new passion: to provide godly influence to my granddaughters.

I had prayed for a godly daughter-in-law. Though the answer came in a different package than I was expecting, God *did* answer my prayer.

A Prayer for You

Father, sometimes I get upset for no reason. My thoughts are anxious and my heart is disquieted. Help me to choose prayer over worry and to experience your peace in the midst of uncertainty. As you work out your will in my life, help me to accept your good gifts in whatever packages they appear. Amen.

A Prayer for Your Grandchild
FOCUS: Courage

O Father, builder of character and courage, may my grandchild grow strong in the light of your face. Grant him courage to stand for what is right, to guard the truth, and to ensure justice in every aspect of life. May he boldly grow in grace, revere your name, and proudly proclaim you as the Lord of Lords and King of Kings.

"Does God Still Love Me?"

"As the Father has loved me, so have I loved you.
Now remain in my love. If you keep my commands,
you will remain in my love, just as I have kept my
Father's commands and remain in his love."
—JOHN 15:9–10

I had been diligently teaching my four-year-old grandson, Max, the importance of obeying me, so he'll always be under the umbrella of my love, as I am under God's love.

The heater was on in my office one cold and rainy winter day while Max was over for a visit. Seizing the opportunity for a teaching moment, I walked him over close to the heater. As I held his little hand in mine, I drew it close enough to the heater to show him how hot it was. Then I clearly explained to him that he should never touch it.

A few days later Max was visiting again. Suddenly I heard a yelp coming from my office. Running over to see what had happened, I discovered that little Max had touched the heater in spite of my careful instructions. His finger was burned. I was very upset. "Why did you touch the heater when I told you not to? Why did you disobey me?" He shyly sighed. Then he said, "I know you love me when I obey you, Nana, but I wanted to find out if you still love me, and if God still loves me, even if I disobey."

By Margaret Fishback Powers

"Isn't it much better to obey me, and remain *in* my love and *in* God's love?" I asked him.

He agreed wholeheartedly, and we both had a little cry. Needless to say, this lesson has guided him regarding his desire to help in the kitchen.

A Prayer for You

Dear loving Father, thank you for loving me continually—when I obey your will and even when I disobey.
Help me to see how precious and secure it is to remain in your love. Amen.

A Prayer for Your Grandchild
FOCUS: Respect for Authority

Dear Lord, I pray that my grandchild will continually grow to respect those in authority. May he learn to be cooperative and fair in work and play. Instill in him a high regard for officials who govern our land and enforce the laws. May his relationships with parents, teachers, coaches, mentors, and bosses be respectful, admirable, constructive, and caring. Amen.

day 19

When We Don't Understand

"The LORD gave and the LORD has taken away;
may the name of the LORD be praised."
—JOB 1:21

Lori glowed with health as she entered the third trimester of pregnancy. I was already a doting grandmother, shopping for a pink layette and baby furniture.

One warm August morning my daughter called on her way to the doctor's office, worried that all was not normal. An hour passed and my phone rang again. With a sob in his voice, my son-in-law Bruce said, "Something has happened to the baby! Can you go to the hospital to be with Lori until I can get there?"

What must my precious daughter be going through? "Oh, God, please uphold and comfort her," I earnestly prayed.

The moment I saw her, weeping and in shock, I knew it was true. My first grandchild was dead. I gathered Lori in my arms, and we sobbed together. *By Rebecca Lutzer*
Our hopes and dreams for our precious bundle of joy were dashed. But I knew that God is faithful and would carry us through our sorrow.

The next day Lori delivered a stillborn baby girl— Sarah. I held her in my arms, desperately wanting to bring her back to life. As the nurse took her away from us, my heart ached for my children. Their loss was so great. It would take months, years, for them to adjust to empty arms and a silent nursery.

I wept for them, not for myself. Bowing my head, I worshiped God in that hospital room. "The LORD gave and the LORD has taken away; may the name of the LORD be praised" (Job 1:21).

A Prayer for You

Sovereign Lord, thank you for the grace to go on when my heart is broken. Help me to trust you even when I don't understand your ways and purposes. Please comfort my children and grandchildren when they go through trials and storms. Amen.

A Prayer for Your Grandchild
FOCUS: Physical Well-Being

Almighty God, Creator of us all, I pray that you will watch over my grandchild's physical development. May she grow in strength through the stages of her life. As she grows in awareness of her body, help her to understand that each body develops uniquely yet is within your plan and your control. Please guard her health so her diseases are few, her injuries are minor, and her infirmities are brief. Amen.

Growing Old Is Not for Wimps

He [whose delight is in the law of the LORD]
shall be like a tree planted by the rivers of water, that
brings forth its fruit in its season, whose leaf also
shall not wither; and whatever he does shall prosper.
—PSALM 1:3 (NKJV)

As I look in the mirror these days, I can't help but notice things are not as they used to be. My face has lines and creases that were not there before. (I refuse to call them wrinkles!) I have puckers and pouches that appear out of nowhere. However, while everything else is succumbing to gravity, I have been consoled by the fact that my eyelashes are thriving. They have been growing so well that they are sweeping the top of my eyelids. This was an exciting development until another discovery crushed my joy. "Dawn," I moaned to

By Dawn Scott Damon

myself as I looked in the mirror, "your eyelashes aren't touching your brow because they're growing; your eyelids are sagging!"

What can I say? Growing old is not for wimps. God has promised, however, that in every season of life we can continue to be fruitful if we follow his antiaging prescription. Psalm 1 says if we delight ourselves in God and meditate on His Word, we will be like a tree planted by the water.

This word picture evokes a powerful image as we envision what that tree looks like. Age does not diminish it but instead increases its value. Its branches are strong and do not waver; its leaves are lush and offer shade; its fruit is plentiful and timely.

No matter our age, our lives—like this tree—will remain fruitful and meaningful when our roots stay planted in the Lord, the living water. We will bear fruit in every season of life, our leaf will not wither or fall away, and we will prosper in all our endeavors.

A Prayer for You

Ageless Father, you alone are the giver and sustainer of life. May my roots be firmly planted in you and your life-giving Word as I am daily renewed. I trust that as I remain planted in you, my life—body, soul, and spirit—will be fruitful and prosperous. In Jesus's name, amen.

A Prayer for Your Grandchild
FOCUS: **Self-Image**

O loving God, I praise you for creating my grandchild as a special, unique individual. Now I ask you to help him appreciate his uniqueness. Build up his self-image so he can enjoy his individuality. Help him to stand for who he is, where he has come from, and what he believes in. Encourage him not only to have hopes and dreams for the future but to also enjoy each day as it comes. In Jesus's name, amen.

day 21

Praise Ribbons

*I will extol the LORD at all times; his praise
will always be on my lips. I will glory in the LORD;
let the afflicted hear and rejoice. Glorify
the LORD with me; let us exalt his name together.*
—PSALM 34:1–3

"Grandma, will you help me make a praise ribbon?"

"A praise ribbon?" Five-year-old Liam meant the color-ful streamers I'd bought from a liturgical dance company. "Oh, honey, you can play with mine. I don't mind."

Liam shook his head. "I want one of my own to take to church on Sunday."

I knew exactly how he felt. From the moment I had seen a group of dancers use the shimmering ribbons to lift ban-ners of praise to God during a worship service, I wanted to worship like that. At my age, it wasn't likely I would become part of a "dance group," but I felt a deep *By Neta Jackson* longing to worship God with my whole being—body, soul, and spirit. So I bought several ribbons, put on a gospel CD at home, and danced my praise to God.

It all started with reading the Psalms during my morn-ing devotions. Psalm 34 begins, "I will extol the LORD at all times . . ." followed by a string of similar words: "praise" . . . "glory in the Lord" . . . "rejoice" . . . "glorify" . . . "exalt his name."

Wait a minute. Did all those words mean the same thing? I looked them up in the dictionary. Each word offered a slightly different meaning. But I was startled by the meaning of *exalt*: "to give lavish praise."

Lavish? As in "over the top," "extravagant," "excessive"? Had I ever given God *lavish* praise? I'd grown up with a lot of no-nos—and moving my body to music was one of them. Only it didn't square with the Bible: "Let them praise his name with dancing" (Psalm 149:3).

So Liam made his own praise ribbon. He took it to church. When the congregation sang their praises to God, he danced and waved his ribbon. Lavish praise.

A Prayer for You

O God, when I think about your faithfulness to my family and me, I want to dance! I want to shout! Because you are a lavish God, I want to give you lavish praise.

A Prayer for Your Grandchild
FOCUS: Worship

Dear Lord, you are worthy of worship. Please guide my grandchild to sense the value of worship, especially corporate worship with other believers in the body of Christ. Help him to know the value of meeting together at church with others who share a love for Jesus Christ, and help him to know that worshiping, learning from God's Word, and gaining insights from other believers at church are vital to his spiritual growth.

day 22

Start Each Day with God

Because he turned his ear to me,
I will call on him as long as I live.
—PSALM 116:2

By the time we've reached this stage in our lives, we should have our priorities in line. One of the great things about the empty-nest years is that we have more time just for ourselves. But even though we have more free time, we must still select the important issues to follow—like starting each day with God. By spending time with God, we grow in the nine aspects of the "fruit of the Spirit": love, joy, peace, forbearance, kindness, goodness, faithfulness, gentleness, and self-control (see Galatians 5:22–23). Which of us doesn't need a touch more of these in our lives?

I've designed part of my walk-in closet as a "prayer closet." It's my favorite spot to get away from everyone and all the distractions. In there, it's just the Lord and me. Beside my special Victorian chair I have a basket full of prayer tools: a Bible, a devotional book, Kleenex, my prayer journal, a packet of note cards, a pen. When I first started *By Emilie Barnes* using my prayer closet, I allotted fifteen minutes to spend with God, but now I often spend an hour with Him. I pray, I listen, I respond to God. When I exit my closet, I feel refreshed, challenged, at peace, and ready to meet the world.

As grandmothers we must ask ourselves, *Are we doing what's important in our day—or only what is urgent?* All of us make choices, and when we don't make time for the most important relationship in our lives, we are probably not making the best choices.

The times and places you meet God will vary, but the fact that you meet alone with Him each day should be a constant in your life. We grandmothers need all the spiritual strength we can get. To keep up with the energy and movement of our kids and their kids, we need to possess the nine elements of the fruit of the Spirit.

A Prayer for You

Father God, may I never forget to call on you in every situation. I want to meet with you every day of my life and bring before you my adoration, confession, thanksgiving, and supplications. Thank you for being willing to be within the sound of my voice and only a thought's distance away. Amen.

A Prayer for Your Grandchild
FOCUS: Protection from Worldliness

O Sovereign Lord, the world surrounds my grandchild, pressing in and tempting him in so many ways. Help him set appropriate limits. Give him sound judgment to choose wisely. Guard him from temptation; protect him from physical and mental predators; lead him into paths of righteousness and light. And reassure me with your promise that you are holding him in your hands. Amen.

day 23

Wing Power

*Those who hope in the LORD will renew
their strength. They will soar on wings like eagles;
they will run and not grow weary,
they will walk and not be faint.*
—ISAIAH 40:31

My grandchildren are quite fascinated with the eagle pictures, sculptures, and photos in their papa's office. They are intrigued as well with his heavy ring displaying two silver eagles on a wide gold band, inscribed with the verse from Isaiah 40:31.

I love to explain to my grandchildren the significance of this verse: It was given as a promise and encouragement by our pastor on the day we were married. As we *By Margaret Fishback Powers* faced burdens in life together, which often came down so heavily we could not carry them any longer, we would pray to God to remove them. However, over the years we discovered that God's plan was to use those burdens to develop "wing power" in our lives.

As we look at the eagles together, I tell my grandchildren about their nature. When the eagles know a storm is coming, they wait until it strikes. Then they face the storm, spread their wings, and rise upward through it. We can be like the eagles, I explain to my grandchildren. When the pressures, burdens, and obstacles of life come upon us, our "prayer power" takes us through the storm and lifts us above it. This prayer strength comes from learning to "wait upon the LORD," as the King James Version renders Isaiah 40:31. I tell them the waiting means complete and habitual trusting and "stick-to-it-ness" in spite of any problems and difficulties that arise.

A while ago I also shared this analogy with a young lad in Great Britain who was feeling very discouraged in his cross-country racing. He had been placing in the bottom section of the races he was in. After taking these words to heart, he is now "soaring and gliding" in the top five.

We must never give in or give up. We must keep trusting, and we will eventually soar.

A Prayer for You

O Lord, help me never to give in or give up. Sustain me with your presence. Uplift me with your strength. Let me see burdens and challenges as opportunities to develop "wing power" in my life, so I may soar above these earthly cares. Amen.

A Prayer for Your Grandchild
FOCUS: Courage

O Father, builder of character and courage, may my grandchild grow strong in the light of your face. Grant him courage to stand for what is right, to guard the truth, and to ensure justice in every aspect of life. May he boldly grow in grace, revere your name, and proudly proclaim you as the Lord of Lords and King of Kings.

day 24

Blessings and Prayers

"Assemble and listen, sons of Jacob;
listen to your father Israel."
—GENESIS 49:2

"I've decided to give a blessing to all my children and grandchildren," announced Oma when she came to visit. "I don't want to wait 'til I'm on my deathbed."

She opened her Bible to Genesis 49 and pulled her granddaughter close. "Jacob blessed his twelve sons before he died," she said. "Now I have asked God to give me a Scripture blessing for each person in our family."

Gently, Oma laid her hand on Beth's head. "For you I have a special Scripture blessing." She smiled, remembering the times she had rescued her adventuresome granddaughter who had climbed too high and couldn't get back down safely. Once she had even rescued Beth from a swarm of bees.

Closing her eyes, Beth solemnly folded her hands.

"He will command his angels concerning you to guard you in all your ways; they will lift you up in their hands, so that you will not strike your foot against a stone" (Psalm 91:11–12). *By Helen Haidle*

Then Oma held up a piece of paper cut in an oval shape. "I've also written a special prayer for you on this paper seed. I pray it for you often. I've planted it like a seed in my Bible. God will answer my prayer. Someday I hope you'll put this 'seed' in your Bible. Every time you read it, remember my blessing and prayers."

Oma shared her idea with other grandmothers. "Blessings and prayers deposit in our grandchildren a sense of being loved—by us and by God," she said. "If our grandchildren know we value them, it gives them a sense of stability. I pray it will also help them trust our faithful God." Remember God's promise: the seeds of his Word always grow and bear fruit (see Isaiah 55:10–11).

A Prayer for You

O Lord, you have blessed me with many blessings. Thank you for letting me bless my family like Jacob blessed his sons. Draw my loved ones close to you. Help me know how to pray for each child and grandchild. Please grow the seeds I plant. For Jesus's sake, amen.

A Prayer for Your Grandchild
FOCUS: Physical Well-Being

Almighty God, Creator of us all, I pray that you will watch over my grandchild's physical development. May she grow in strength through the stages of her life. As she grows in awareness of her body, help her to understand that each body develops uniquely yet is within your plan and your control. Please guard her health so her diseases are few, her injuries are minor, and her infirmities are brief. Amen.

day 25

The Pickle Party

With this in mind, we constantly pray for you,
that our God may make you worthy of his calling,
and that by his power he may bring
to fruition your every desire for goodness
and your every deed prompted by faith.
—2 THESSALONIANS 1:11

We were delighted to discover that our hotel lived up to the description in the brochure. Hannah soon made a discovery. "Grammy," she exclaimed, "there's a bathtub big enough to be a pool in your bedroom! Let's go swimming!"

The next day we donned our swimming suits and filled the tub with water. I stacked pickles on a plate, and we called our Jacuzzi outing "The Pickle Party." In between our chatter, we took turns picking dill pickles off the plate as we munched our way through the next hour.

By Carol Kent

"Hannah," I said, "what's the best part of today?"

Her response was right on: "Talking to each other about being a woman is *definitely* the best part of today."

"How do you think I can help you best, Hannah?" I asked.

"Well," she said, admiring her image in the big mirror next to the tub, "I think you can teach me how to be a good mom."

"Hannah," I said, "Grammy's been praying for your future husband."

Her eyes grew big, and she laughed. "It's too early to pray for my husband, Grammy. I'm just a kid."

I piled soapy hair on top of her head in a coiffure as I said, "It's never too early to pray about whom you're going to marry. It's one of the most important decisions of your life."

"Well, that's not going to happen for a long time," she stated emphatically, "but thanks for praying for me." Then, chomping down on her sixth dill pickle, she abruptly decided we had taken enough time for adult discussion, and it was time to play.

We made a memory that day—Grammy and Hannah— as we had a pickle party while talking about growing up and the necessity of prayer.

A Prayer for You

Father, thank you for the opportunity I have to pray for my grandchildren in the area of your design for marriage and family—and for the opportunities I have to share with them and talk about their family and spouses (current or future). Help me to use every opportunity to instill your principles into our conversations, so living a life based on your Word becomes the most natural way for my grandchildren to live. Amen.

A Prayer for Your Grandchild
FOCUS: Spiritual Growth

Dear Lord, today I pray for my grandchild's spiritual growth. I ask that you instill in him the desire to read and memorize your Word. Give him a passion to be in conversation with you. May loving and serving you be part of his daily life. I ask that you stay close to him and lead him to be transformed to your likeness, to reflect your grace, and to radiate your love. I pray this in Jesus's name, amen.

day 26

"You're a Sparkler"

When the angel of the LORD appeared to Gideon,
he said, "The LORD is with you, mighty warrior."
—JUDGES 6:12

We can learn a lot about the power of spoken words from the angel who spoke to a frightened man named Gideon. The angel set a wonderful example for us to follow with our grandchildren.

Showing up is the first thing to do. The angel appeared at the place where Gideon was hiding. Where do you go to meet your grandchild? His soccer game, her gymnastics meet, the kitchen table, *By Bobbie Wolgemuth* the hallway of your church, the phone? Find a place to applaud a child with your presence.

Next look at what the angel said about God. "The Lord is with you" (Judges 6:12). One of our family's favorite goodbye lines to say over the phone or when we part company with each other is, "The Lord be with you." It is a simple way to assure someone that God is always a companion close at hand.

Then the angel called Gideon a "mighty warrior." A seed was planted in his heart . . . a thought of potential identity. Until then Gideon most likely hadn't thought of himself as a soldier—especially not a mighty one.

I learned how a simple phrase has the potential to foster identity when my grandson, Luke, was coloring at the kitchen table one day. He surprised me with a creative picture, and I exclaimed, "Luke, you're an artist!" I didn't think anything else about the comment until two days later when Luke was on the floor with art paper and markers around him. When I came to look at his newest project, Luke said, "You're right, Nanny, I *am* an artist!"

To bless your grandchildren, it's easy to follow this pattern. Show up where they are, tell them that the Lord is with them, and give them a strong word of identity.

Speaking something as simple as, "You're a sparkler," may cause a child to shine brighter than ever.

A Prayer for You

Lord, thank you for showing up with words of hope and identity every day. I want to bless my grandchildren with my presence and by speaking simple words of encouragement to them. Amen.

A Prayer for Your Grandchild
FOCUS: Self-Image

O loving God, I praise you for creating my grandchild as a special, unique individual. Now I ask you to help her appreciate her uniqueness. Build up her self-image so she can enjoy her individuality. Help her to stand for who she is, where she has come from, and what she believes in. Encourage her not only to have hopes and dreams for the future but also to enjoy each day as it comes. In Jesus's name, amen.

The Face of an Angel

All who were sitting in the Sanhedrin
looked intently at Stephen,
and they saw that his face was like
the face of an angel.
—ACTS 6:15

Grandmother was beaming with radiance. Her face shone with an indescribable glow. Her skin was smooth; her hands, once bent and arthritic, were resting relaxed and easy. She was passing from this life to the next, and she was beautiful—like a bride ready to meet her groom.

It was nothing like I had expected. I thought I would be uncomfortable facing death—that there would be nervousness and fear. But that day *By Dawn Scott Damon* when I entered my grandmother's room to say farewell and to tell her that I loved her, I was instantly enveloped by an immense peace. The presence of God's comfort lingered in the air like a thick cloud.

Wondering why her countenance was so peaceful, I remembered the story of Stephen's martyrdom. Even his accusers saw that his face "was like the face of an angel" (Acts 6:15). And then just before the angry mob stoned him to death, "Stephen, full of the Holy Spirit, looked up to heaven and saw the glory of God, and Jesus standing at the right hand of God" (Acts 7:55). I wondered if Stephen, before he died, looked like Grandma did now. That's when it hit me: Death for the believer—for those whose sins are forgiven—is the most precious and intimate experience one will have with God. His presence is never closer.

Psalm 116:15 declares: "Precious in the sight of the LORD is the death of his faithful servants." We are so valuable to the Lord that He watches over our life and even our death with great care and compassion. His peace will never leave us. His love will not forsake us. Nothing can separate us from God—not even death.

Standing in Grandma's room that day, a song filled my heart: "In mansions of glory and endless delight, I'll ever adore Thee in heaven so bright; I'll sing with the glittering crown on my brow: If ever I loved Thee, my Jesus, 'tis now." Grandma's hand extended to the heavens in worship. An ever so slight smile appeared . . . and her face was like the face of an angel.

A Prayer for You

Precious Lord, thank you for your promise to never leave me or forsake me. Help me to live in the knowledge of your ever-abiding presence and power every day. I choose to lean on you—the Love that casts out all fear—and rest in your unfailing compassion. Amen.

A Prayer for Your Grandchild
FOCUS: Salvation

Dear Lord, please guide my grandchild to your gift of salvation. I pray that he will come to know you, love you, and to walk close to you throughout his life. May he boldly claim Jesus as his Lord and Savior. Guide him as he makes choices that have eternal consequences. Help him to follow you each moment of his life. I pray this in Jesus's name, amen.

day 28

A Stronghold of Protection

*Through the praise of children and infants
you have established a stronghold against your
enemies, to silence the foe and the avenger.*

—PSALM 8:2

Walking my grandson to preschool, which I do about once a week, is a far different experience than my "exercise walks." The first time we started out, I thought it would take us fifteen minutes, even considering shorter legs. Uh-uh. Double that.

A five-year-old is delighted by all he sees. He carefully picks dandelion bouquets for his teacher, for his mom, for me. He examines the stem of one and wonders, "Why did God make that gooey white stuff inside?" (I'd *By Neta Jackson* never noticed dandelion stems had gooey white stuff inside. Imagine that.) We pause to admire purple tulips, knots in tree trunks, ants building anthills in sidewalk cracks.

The world is a wonder to a child, and he has no trouble at all assigning all the credit to God's handiwork.

So that's how I first read Psalm 8, praising God with childlike wonder for His awesome creation, especially the vast expanse of a nighttime sky, with its moon and stars and galaxies far, far away. But recently, verse two startled me: the praise of children silences the enemy. Wow! That's some pretty powerful praise! But if the praise of children and infants can silence the enemy, then my praise is also important spiritual warfare.

The more I meditate on this Scripture, the more it makes sense. Satan's work thrives in an atmosphere of doubt, worry, distraction, busyness, and discouragement. But praise? Praise to the living God is not Satan's working condition. If I want to build a stronghold of protection against that old devil, I need to fill my heart, my thoughts, and my home with praise!

A Prayer for You

Creator God, your wonderful works surround me—in nature, in my life, in the world at large—in spite of horrific world events that confirm Satan is bent on disruption and destruction. But, O God, let my praise to you be a shield and a defense. Amen.

A Prayer for Your Grandchild
FOCUS: Courage

O Father, builder of character and courage, may my grandchild grow strong in the light of your face. Grant him courage to stand for what is right, to guard the truth, and to ensure justice in every aspect of life. May he boldly grow in grace, revere your name, and proudly proclaim you as the Lord of Lords and King of Kings.

day 29

Granny and God

The king gave this order to all the people:
"Celebrate the Passover to the LORD your God,
as it is written in this Book of the Covenant."
—2 KINGS 23:21

Granny, my father's mother, lived across the driveway from our family. As children, my sister and I ran up her wooden back stairs at least a half a dozen times a day.

On weekends, we would spend the night at Granny's house. She placed a rollaway cot at the end of her bed, insisting that my sister and I kneel beside her to pray. We called out the names of every relative, church member, neighbor, and friend—asking God's blessing. When Granny said good night, we climbed up on the cot. But she stayed on her knees. I watched her mouth moving long into the night. I wondered, what is she saying to God? What secrets did the two of them share?

Now that I'm a grandmother, I can understand why Granny spent time on her knees. Sometimes I shock myself with how long I agonize before the Father on behalf of my family, especially my young grandson Ian. *By Victoria McAfee* I get so concerned because this present world is so godless and upside down. What will it look like in twenty years when little Ian is an adult? I'm praying he becomes one of God's change agents instead of being swallowed up in all the craziness and chaos.

73

God used a little boy, Josiah, to be one of those change agents. He became king over Judah at eight years old (2 Kings 22:1). When he stepped into this leadership role, the people had no idea of their sin. The Scriptures lay locked in the temple. The priest found the book of the law and read it to this young king. Josiah was deeply grieved over how far his people had drifted away from God (2 Kings 22:11–13). He courageously destroyed idols and turned the nation back to God (2 Kings 23:4–27).

A Prayer for You

Lord, raise up my grandsons and granddaughters to be like Josiah. Call them to be strong leaders—helping others to walk steadfast and take a biblical stand.

A Prayer for Your Grandchild
FOCUS: Character

Dear Lord and Father, I ask that you fill my grandchild with your Spirit so her character reflects your goodness and love. Give her kindness and love for others. Bring joy to her life so she will be a joy to others. Grant her patience and self-control through difficult and trying times. May she show mercy and generosity to those who are less fortunate. Grant her integrity and a sense of justice, and surround her with your peace. Amen.

day 30

Creative Spirit

"I have filled him with the Spirit of God,
with wisdom, with understanding,
with knowledge and with all kinds of skills."
—EXODUS 31:3

I love Exodus 31:3. It inspires me. I love the idea that the Spirit of God infused these guys with the skills, abilities, and knowledge to build God's tabernacle, the epoch of all artwork until the later construction of Solomon's temple. And the materials they were given! It gives a crafty person like me shivers of joy to think of it.

The Scriptures don't talk about human creativity much, but perhaps that's because it's a given. After all, we are made in the image of our Creator, who crafted the beautiful and intriguing things of our world: sunsets, stars, trees, beaches, oceans, flamingos, armadillos, strawberries, honeybees, our exquisitely complex bodies, and, of course, life itself. And He has instilled in men and women throughout time the urge to create—from *By Ruth A. DeJager* the cave paintings of ancient people to the psalms of David to the building of cathedrals to the invention of the printing press and beyond.

We tend to think of creativity as having to do with art, but one can be creative in almost any area of life. Creativity is a useful and necessary tool in business, medicine, housekeeping, and even in the nurturing of a grandchild. And to do all these things creatively, inspired by the Spirit of God, is to use our gifts in His service.

It's easy to lose sight of our God-given creativity in the blur of routine and the drudgery of daily life. Sometimes we need to get away on what Julia Cameron, author of *The Artist's Way*, calls an "artist date." That may involve taking a class or a vacation, going for a hike in the woods, or sipping a mocha at the bookstore. Use the time to tune in to your creativity and to re-create your openness to new ways of thinking, feeling, and doing. Listen to the Spirit of God telling you how to be creative in your own unique way.

A Prayer for You

Creator of all things, thank you for the creative gifts you have given me. Help me to discover the creative gifts still hidden within me. And grant me the wisdom to nurture the creative gifts within my grandchildren as well. Amen.

A Prayer for Your Grandchild
FOCUS: Talents

Dear Lord, the giver of gifts, bless my grandchild as she develops her talents. Help her identify her talents and be proud and confident of the gifts you have given her. Give her patience and understanding, Lord, so she will not grow weary of striving and searching to reach the goals you have set for her. May each milestone bring satisfaction and a healthy desire for greater achievement and success to bring glory to you. Amen.

day 31

Commemoration

*"This is a day you are to commemorate;
for the generations to come you shall celebrate it
as a festival to the LORD—a lasting ordinance."*
—EXODUS 12:14

My grandmother on my mom's side died at age forty-five. But Grandma Doris spent her last months in joyful celebration, working with my mom to plan her wedding. Grandma Doris had five children, and my mother was the oldest. The two were very close. When it became clear that cancer would win the *By Karen Kingsbury* battle for Grandma Doris's life, she refused to stay in a hospital bed.

Instead she spent her time looking through magazines for bridal dresses and dreaming with my mom about flowers and color schemes and, ultimately, my mother's wedding dress. With frail fingers, my Grandma Doris helped my mom button up her wedding gown as she tried it on for the first time. She marveled at the beautiful woman my mother had become, and she prayed at night for God's blessings on my mother's marriage.

My parents' wedding was beautiful, and though Grandma Doris was very ill, she can be seen in the grainy video clips greeting guests and smiling with her whole heart. My parents returned from their honeymoon and helped care for Grandma Doris until she died, six months later. But Doris's prayers have been answered in a dramatic way. My parents' marriage was very strong; they had been married forty-five years when my dad died in 2007. When we celebrated their wedding anniversary, it was always with a special thought for Grandma Doris and the lasting value of her love shown on that special wedding date.

In addition, I included a picture of my Grandma Doris and my mother through my novel *Reunion*. The fictitious story of Elizabeth Baxter and her daughter Ashley is a tribute, in many ways, to the love my Grandma Doris had for her children, especially the love she showed my mother in the days before her wedding.

A Prayer for You

Dear Lord, there is something special about a grandmother's love, something that brings generations together. Thank you for this time with the people we love. Thank you that we can commemorate those we love during special celebrations and times of remembrance. Amen.

A Prayer for Your Grandchild
FOCUS: Relationships at Home

O Lord, I pray that you will bless the home and family of my grandchild. May the relationships he has with his parents and siblings enhance his well-being, support his self-confidence, and increase his faith. May his home life reflect your love, your grace, your compassion, and your peace. Guide his parents to direct him in love and truth, so he will grow into a strong and compassionate individual. Amen.

READ MATTHEW 6:25–34

day 32

Seek First His Kingdom

*"But seek first his kingdom
and his righteousness,
and all these things will be given
to you as well."*
—MATTHEW 6:33

"Mom, I'm pregnant."

The words hung in the air—part statement, part anxious question—as my sixteen-year-old daughter searched my face, waiting for my reaction.

I was stunned.

What about all of my dreams for her: the college diploma and the brilliant career?

Then my dreams for my own life rudely pushed their way to the forefront of my thoughts. My husband and I had placed so many things on hold for the last twenty years. Shouldn't it be our turn to do the things we wanted? As we talked through the situation, I knew that my daughter's words revealed the probable course of my next twenty years. I was exhausted just from thinking about the demands of raising a baby, a toddler, and eventually a teenager!

By Debby Kerner Rettino

My daughter gave the best effort she could at being a mom, but she was too young and not equipped for all of the demands of raising a child. So she did the best thing she knew how to do: She asked us if we would take care of our grandson. We could not say no.

Yes, there were plenty of times when I longed to sleep in rather than get a first-grader to school. Now, as he enters adolescence, battling over homework and checking on whom he is hanging out with wear me out. When I feel like I am going down for the third time with fatigue and frustration, I recall that God provides for all my needs as I seek Him first. Just as He takes care of the birds and wild-flowers, God gives me the stamina and stick-to-itiveness to parent my grandchild. I accept God's strength, and I rejoice as I cheer at soccer games, cuddle during bedtime stories, and accept the awkward kiss of a young teenager heading to his first dance.

Those are the gifts of grandmothering and the blessings of God in my life.

A Prayer for You

Father in heaven, I acknowledge that you are all-powerful. It is only through your Son, Jesus, that I can have righteousness and the hope of heaven. Thank you that your kingdom is not only in the future, but it is right now, and you, my source, are able to provide everything I need. When I am weak, I trust you to give me strength. When I am discouraged, I trust you to give me joy. When I am inadequate, I trust you to be enough. Help me to turn to you first. I pray this in the powerful name of Jesus.

A Prayer for Your Grandchild
FOCUS: Emotional Development

O God, Creator of mind and body, I pray that you will give my grandchild emotional health and strength. Where there is anger, bring peace. Where there is confusion, bring clarity and focus. Where there are dark shadows, cast a ray of hope. Fill her with the sunshine of your Spirit. Warm her with the presence of your peace. In Jesus's name, amen.

You're Not Alone

"I went away full, but the LORD
has brought me back empty."
—RUTH 1:21

My fifty-nine-year-old husband, Steve, lost his valiant battle with colon cancer. Now, like many of you, I'm traveling the path I never wanted: the widow's walk. When I bought my first car alone, a silver Honda, my nine-year-old grandson, Simeon, said:

"Grandma, you should name this car the Silver Bullet."

I smiled. "I've already named it the Grey Goose."

"Why?"

"Because when the mate of a grey goose dies, the other flies on alone for the rest of her life."

Simeon looked at me tenderly. "You aren't alone, Grandma; you've got us."

Tears welled up in my eyes. It's true. And how thankful I am.

When Naomi lost her husband and sons, she came home to an empty house, haunted by *By Dee Brestin* their absence. She said, "I went away full, but the LORD has brought me back empty" (Ruth 1:21).

After burying Steve, coming home was one of the hardest things I'd ever done. Each room I wandered through cried, "Empty!" I felt *so* alone.

Yet, in truth, we aren't alone. Not only will the Lord never leave us but we are also still blessed with family. Naomi had her daughter-in-law Ruth, who committed her whole life to Naomi with her famous "Where you go I will go" (Ruth 1:16). At the close of the book, when Naomi was cradling her newborn grandson, the women of Bethlehem praised the Lord for not leaving Naomi alone. The Lord had given Naomi not only a daughter-in-law who was "better to [her] than seven sons" (Ruth 4:15) but also now a grandson who would grow up to love her and care for her.

As Simeon said to me, "You're not alone, Grandma; you've got us."

A Prayer for You

Father, help me to be thankful for my grandchildren. Help me not to dwell on what I've lost but to be thankful for what I still have.

A Prayer for Your Grandchild
FOCUS: Courage

O Father, builder of character and courage, may my grandchild grow strong in the light of your face. Grant him courage to stand for what is right, to guard the truth, and to ensure justice in every aspect of life. May he boldly grow in grace, revere your name, and proudly proclaim you as the Lord of Lords and King of Kings.

day 34

A Family Place

*When she and the members of her household
were baptized, she invited us to her home.
"If you consider me a believer in the Lord," she said,
"come and stay at my house." And she persuaded us.*
—ACTS 16:15

I love our home. It's a family home. It's a place where all our children and their children, with their friends, can come and be at ease. Even though I have some very nice "stuff," there's no room that's off-limits to them. The only chair they can't sit in is Papaw's green La-Z-Boy. The kids love to sit in it anyway, just to hear him say, "Git out'a my chair, little gal." He likes to sit there and hold the babies on his lap while the other kids run around the house singing, playing, dancing, creating things, teasing each other, and asking Papaw if they can have juice out of the little handy refrigerator he bought so they could get their own drinks.

When I look around and see the fingerprints, crayon marks, broken toys, juice spots,

By Thelma Wells

pieces of paper, sticky glue, jelly stains, diapers, and bottles, I think, "Boy, there's really no place like home." It's total chaos, but it's great!

It's not always chaos. Sometimes it gets downright serious when we begin to answer the children's questions or have character-building discussions. We teach them to

84

pray, say grace, recite Bible verses, and respect our country, community, and other people. They learn to share and get along with others and to clean up what they mess up. As parents and grandparents, we are given a charge to make our houses homes of love and learning.

Is your house a home? Does your family feel welcome? Will people remember fond memories of being there? When your children leave, will they want to come back and bring their kids with them? Will they be able to say with joy in their hearts, "There's no place like home"?

A Prayer for You

Thank you, Lord, for the gift and blessing of a home. May mine be a place of laughing, loving, and learning—a place where others, especially my children and grandchildren, can always feel "at home." In Jesus's name, amen.

A Prayer for Your Grandchild
FOCUS: Relationships at Home

O Lord, I pray that you will bless the home and family of my grandchild. May the relationships he has with his parents and siblings enhance his well-being, support his self-confidence, and increase his faith. May his home life reflect your love, your grace, your compassion, and your peace. Guide his parents to direct him in love and truth, so he will grow into a strong and compassionate individual. Amen.

day 35

I Will . . . I Will . . .

I will give thanks to you, LORD, with all my heart;
I will tell of all your wonderful deeds.
I will be glad and rejoice in you;
I will sing the praises of your name, O Most High.
—PSALM 9:1–2

Psalm 9 contains a great "I Will" activity list to remember to do when you spend time with your grandchild.

First, start with an attitude of praise. Tell the Lord what you are thankful for. Count your blessings; name them. It will be easy to have a heart full of thankfulness after you've named even a few. Your heart will be full and running over with the kind of attitude that pleases God and spills over on the young ones with the love of the Savior.

Second, tell the kids what God has done in the past. One of our greatest resources as grandmothers is the history we have lived. Tell your grandchild about the time his mother was a little girl and was sick or lost in the department store or scared to go to school and the way God provided a solution to the problem. Everyday miracles fill our memory banks. Pull a few past marvels out of your memory treasure chest, and tell your grandchild of the Lord's wonders.

By Bobbie Wolgemuth

Third, be a happy grandmother. Open the door with a smile and a hug. Let your face show the gladness of the Lord. Your inside joy should envelop your grandchildren with every encounter, no matter where you are. They should want to be around you just because they feel your ecstasy and love. Remember to smile and laugh often with them.

The fourth "I will" is my favorite: sing. Sing with your grandchildren. Teach them the words of a hymn. They hear and remember rhyming lines so quickly that in no time they can memorize inspired verses. Leave a song in their hearts. It will bring them truth and comfort and peace for a lifetime. Remember to sing aloud every day.

A Prayer for You

Lord Jesus, I want to be the kind of grandmother who encourages others. Help me today to do your will by remembering the four "I Will" statements in Psalm 9. I want to praise, tell, rejoice, and sing. Amen.

A Prayer for Your Grandchild
FOCUS: Spiritual Growth

Dear Lord, today I pray for my grandchild's spiritual growth. I ask that you instill in her the desire to read and memorize your Word. Give her a passion to be in conversation with you. May loving and serving you be part of her daily life. I ask that you stay close to her and lead her to be transformed to your likeness, to reflect your grace, and to radiate your love. I pray this in Jesus's name, amen.

day 36

Make the Monsters Go Away!

When you lie down,
you will not be afraid;
when you lie down,
your sleep will be sweet.
—PROVERBS 3:24

One night I was babysitting our five-year-old grandson, Lyden, when he woke from a troubling dream.

"Mama Quin!" he screamed. "How do I get these monsters to go away?" he asked as he bolted upright in his bed.

"Just ask Jesus to make them go away," I answered. "He says He never leaves us. In fact, the Bible says God has angels watching over you. So you can go back to sleep."

"Oh, okay—is that all?" he asked. I prayed a short prayer, asking God to protect Lyden from nightmares and thanking Him for His watchful care. Lyden repeated the prayer after me. Then he rolled over and fell asleep again.

When we grandmothers aren't bashful about praying aloud in front of our grandchildren, we are actually teaching them how to pray. As we inter-

By Quin Sherrer

cede for them, we beseech God to move on their behalf. Other times, we find ourselves saying no to the adversary's tactics to harass and tempt them. The Scriptures are our arsenal, our prayer manual, and our book of promises. As our grandchildren hear us pray, they can come to understand that even they can stand against the powers of darkness. They just need to call on the Lord, their deliverer.

Grandchildren just seem to trust their grandmas. And grandmas trust their God.

A Prayer for You

Heavenly Father, help me develop a lifestyle of praying with my grandchildren. May my example encourage and teach them to be intercessors. Thank you that we can trust you as our God of strength and deliverance. Amen.

A Prayer for Your Grandchild
FOCUS: Respect for Authority

Dear Lord, I pray that my grandchild will continually grow to respect those in authority. May she learn to be cooperative and fair in work and at play. Instill in her a high regard for officials who govern our land and enforce the laws. May her relationships with parents, teachers, coaches, mentors, and bosses be respectful, admirable, constructive, and caring. Amen.

day 37

Beauty in Busy Hands

Every skilled woman spun with her hands and
brought what she had spun—blue, purple or scarlet
yarn or fine linen. And all the women who were
willing and had the skill spun the goat hair.
—EXODUS 35:25–26

Have you recently noticed the creative art of God? Color, texture, arrangement, unique design, and images of beauty are everywhere.

Made in God's image, women have been gifted with a capacity to generate and display beauty. Any expression that brings loveliness into the world exposes the artist's soul and is a visible reminder that God is the master designer.

A vase with a single flower on the table, a pretty scarf around the neck, vegetables and fruit arranged on a plate, a burst of color planted in the garden, a watercolor painting, or some pretty yarn knit into a shawl . . . there's no limit to the variety of creative expressions that can stir our souls.

By Bobbie Wolgemuth

Recently my granddaughter asked me to teach her how to crochet. It's one of the old crafts coming back into fashion for young people. After visiting a craft store and selecting hooks and brightly colored yarn, I asked the clerk to give me a refresher course. It had been years since I had crocheted, but her kindness and simple instructions were all I needed.

My granddaughter and I sat on the sofa together. Busy hands worked the yarn as good conversation wove our hearts together.

God has gifted us with good ideas. And when we share our skills and art with our family, our lives can be woven together. Maybe it's time for you to listen to the creative stirring in your soul. Busy hands can arrange beauty and blend hearts. What artistic project can you try—or try again—today?

A Prayer for You

Father in heaven, thank you for beauty. Thank you for the inspiration to try new projects. Help me to enjoy what you have provided. Give me wisdom to share art and loveliness with my grandchildren. Amen.

A Prayer for Your Grandchild
FOCUS: Creativity

Lord, you are the master of creativity. You wove this universe into its beautiful existence with just a word, and when you did, you splashed spectacular wonder throughout. But even more, you allowed us to contribute to the beauty of the world with the skills you gave us to create new and lovely things. Guide my grandchild to embrace his creativity and to use it for your praise.

day 38

Your Special Gift

Do not neglect your gift,
which was given you through prophecy
when the body of elders
laid their hands on you.
—1 TIMOTHY 4:14

The makeup of what we call family has changed, but not that much. There has always been "extended" family—those who are special additions. I've got three grandchildren like that. But don't you tell me they're not my own, oh no! I believe I have the gift of surrogate grandmothering. And I never take it for granted.

Before Destiny and Israel, there was Dionne. She's my stepgrandbaby. Her freckled face could outshine the sun. She and I would play dolls and run and frolic in the autumn leaves. Her presence in the Rambo home added more love. Now she's a talented lady with a wonderful husband and child of her own. Dyson's my first great-grandbaby!

Then after Destiny and Israel came two babies who kept me young. Although they have their own grand-mothers, Christian and Pierce live close by. They're the two bright boys of my manager, Larry. They sang and played silly games with me while they keep on growing. Somehow in the middle of helping keep an eye on them, they entwined themselves into my heart.

By Dottie Rambo

That's so like God. While we're busy with our plans, He comes along and taps on our shoulder. He whispers in our ear, "If you could help out with this one . . ." And another one is grafted onto the family tree.

A Prayer for You

God, while I'm living my day-to-day life, help me to keep my ears open and my gifts at the ready for you. In the precious name of Jesus, amen.

A Prayer for Your Grandchild
FOCUS: Relationships at Home

O Lord, I pray that you will bless the home and family of my grandchild. May the relationships she has with her parents and siblings enhance her well-being, support her self-confidence, and increase her faith. May her home life reflect your love, your grace, your compassion, and your peace. Guide her parents to direct her in love and truth so she will grow into a strong and compassionate individual. Amen.

day 39

A Force to Be Reckoned With

*The prayer of a righteous person
is powerful and effective.*
—JAMES 5:16

My eyes slowly fluttered open. The soft, rhythmic sound of Grandma's voice echoed through the early morning, awakening my senses. It was summer vacation in Elkhart, Indiana, and all of us in Grandma and Grandpa's country farmhouse were still sleeping—everyone but Grandma, that is. She was in the kitchen enjoying a private conversation. "Who's she talking to?" my little girl curiosity wondered. I listened intently, but Grandma's sweet tone was the only voice I could

By Dawn Scott Damon

hear. Whoever this mystery person was, she knew him well, for she was sharing her deepest secrets with this patient listener and finding great joy and strength in their time together.

I soon discovered that Grandma was a prayer warrior. It was her practice to rise early in the morning and engage God in conversation. She did not speak with the eloquence of a skilled orator; rather, her dialogue was simple, honest, and determined. She opened up her heart and poured its contents at the feet of Jesus. Grandma's prayers were powerful. She pursued God, and things happened.

God's Word says in James 5:16 that the prayers of the righteous—those living in *right standing* with God—get effective, powerful results. That Scripture means that the prayers of one whose life is right before God make up a mighty force to be reckoned with! The secret of success in prayer is not in our choice of vocabulary but in our relationship with Christ. When our prayers and petitions flow out of a pure heart, we should expect to see mountains move, situations change, and lives transform. Grandma was a force to be reckoned with. We can be too!

A Prayer for You

Precious Lord, thank you for the privilege of talking to you personally and for the promise that you will hear and answer my prayers. Today I bring you all the concerns and requests of my heart. I trust you to meet every need according to your plan and purpose. Amen.

A Prayer for Your Grandchild
FOCUS: Prayer

Gracious Father, thank you for the avenue of prayer. Holy Spirit, please instill within the heart of my grandchild the desire to talk with you in prayer, to be open and transparent with you, and to trust you enough to share his cares, prayers, and concerns.

day 40

Grandma's Lap

Dear friends, let us love one another,
for love comes from God. Everyone who loves
has been born of God and knows God.
—1 JOHN 4:7

"Grandma, you are so comfortable," my grandson said as he snuggled on my lap and rested his head on the soft underside of my upper arm. "Why is that?" I asked. "Because you are so squishy," he answered. I like his perspective. The image in the mirror tells me I could stand to lose more than a few pounds. But my grandson complained when I shed enough pudge that he could feel bones beneath my comfy cushioning.

My grandkids know they are safe and loved when they are sitting on Grandma's lap. In turn, my grandchildren show me they love me by making me drawings, buying me oversized costume jewelry at school fairs, and giving me baby-wet kisses. I repay the compliments by keeping the drawings where everybody can admire them, by proudly wearing the oversized costume jewelry to work, and by relishing grandbaby slobber. Our family is composed of a variety

By Debby Kerner Rettino

of religious and non-religious persuasions, and I might be the best example of the love of Christ my grandkids will know.

When I admire my granddaughter's poetry or wonder at the ability of my young grandson to make stop-frame animation, they know I am their cheerleader. In my eyes, my granddaughter's poetry is the most beautiful in the world, and surely my grandson has a future in video technology! They cannot see God, but they can see me, and they can feel the unconditional love I have for them. This love comes from God.

So what if I don't measure up to a magazine model's ideal. I am the perfect size to be a welcoming, squishy, living gospel and a comfy place for my grandchildren to relax—knowing they are loved.

A Prayer for You

Give me spiritual eyes to see, Lord. Help me to know that I am your hands and feet and lap. I pray this in the powerful name of Jesus.

A Prayer for Your Grandchild
FOCUS: Physical Well-Being

Almighty God, Creator of us all, I pray that you will watch over my grandchild's physical development. May she grow in strength through the stages of her life. As she grows in awareness of her body, help her to understand that each body develops uniquely yet is within your plan and your control. Please guard her health so her diseases are few, her injuries are minor, and her infirmities are brief. Amen.

day 41

Prayers for Bella

"Ask and it will be given to you;
seek and you will find;
knock and the door will be opened to you."
—MATTHEW 7:7

Just as my grandmother's faith in a prayer-answering God was passed down to me, I have seen the same grace of God in my own offspring. A great example of that is my granddaughter, Claire, who was six years old when she learned firsthand about God's faithfulness.

Claire had a Persian cat named Bella, which she loved dearly and that had become part of the family. Imagine the pain in Claire's little heart when she discovered one day that the cat was missing. In the midst of people coming in and out of the house on Christmas Eve, the front door was left open long enough for Bella to curiously wander outside. The outside world of Roslyn, New York, in the dead of winter is no place for a delicate cat like Bella, and the family's hopes of retrieving her dimmed as the days passed.

By Carol Cymbala

Although they scoured the neighborhood and posted signs everywhere, Bella seemed to be gone forever. Claire cried daily over the loss of her precious feline.

Eight days after Bella's disappearance, my son-in-law Brian was putting his daughter to bed, and Claire had a chance to pray aloud. Suddenly she began to pour her broken heart out to God, and she pleaded for the return of her cat. Her prayer was desperate and filled with childlike faith that God has promised to answer.

The next morning, Claire's teacher called my daughter Susan and reported that she was almost sure she had spotted Bella in her backyard. Susan and Claire rushed over, and there was Bella, safe and sound, although worn by the extreme weather and outdoor conditions. When my granddaughter saw her cat, she started jumping and crying out, "Mommy, God really answered my prayer!" What an illustration to my granddaughter's impressionable heart and mind! God still answers prayer!

A Prayer for You

Lord, may we all come before you with the faith of a child. We thank you today that you are the same yesterday, today, and forever and that your ear is ever open to the cries of your children. Our faith and trust are in you and you alone. Amen.

A Prayer for Your Grandchild
FOCUS: Prayer

Gracious Father, thank you for the avenue of prayer. Holy Spirit, please instill within the heart of my grandchild the desire to talk with you in prayer—to be open and transparent with you and to trust you enough to share his cares, prayers, and concerns.

day 42

The Sands of Time

*"I will surely bless you and make your
descendants as numerous as the stars in the sky
and as the sand on the seashore."*
—GENESIS 22:17

Hand in hand, my husband and I walk along the beach. We relax. Beaches do that to us. It's like our eyes and ears are opened—and our hearts. We pause to appreciate the rolling waves, the seagulls flying above, the birds standing on one leg. At times like this, life slows down. We look at each other through the filter of so many years of being best friends and soul mates.

But then Dave and I are joined by our son, daughter-in-law, and Lily, our twelve-month-old granddaughter—and an amazing thing happens. Lily sees the beach for the very first time. The glee. The delight. Her parents revel in the wonder of it all. It's a magical moment. As we reflect on our son and daughter-in-law, we realize that they are much better prepared to be parents, better prepared to build a marriage, than we were at their age. And then we realize that life goes forward, not backward, and just as constant as the sands of time, our heavenly Father goes forward with us. Just as constant as the waves of the ocean, His love will always encompass us.

By Claudia Arp

We think of our other sons, their wives, our grand-children, including precious Lily, who was named after her great-grandmother Lillian—Dave's mother, who several years ago passed on from this life to a better one. Yet even now Dave can remember his parents, in years gone by, walking on the beach, hand in hand. Then he was the child. Today he's the husband, the dad, the grand-dad. Now is the time to invest in future generations. We wonder—will Lily one day walk on this beach with her granddaughter?

A Prayer for You

Lord, may I realize that with the passing of time,
I can pass on a godly heritage to my children and
grandchildren. Please help me be a positive model,
and may I leave a positive path for them to follow
in the sands of time.

A Prayer for Your Grandchild
FOCUS: Salvation

Dear Lord, please guide my grandchild to your gift
of salvation. I pray that she will come to know you, to
love you, and to walk close to you throughout her life.
May she boldly claim Jesus as her Lord and Savior.
Guide her as she makes choices that have eternal
consequences. Help her to follow you each moment
of her life. I pray this in Jesus's name, amen.

The Epitaph

*Jehoram was thirty-two years old when he became
king, and he reigned in Jerusalem eight years.
He passed away, to no one's regret, and was buried in
the City of David, but not in the tombs of the kings.*
—2 CHRONICLES 21:20

"He passed away, to no one's regret."

You've got to be kidding! At first read, this seems almost comical. But after thinking about it for a few moments, one can clearly see that this is a short, sad commentary on someone's life. No one would want an epitaph on her grave marker that read: she died, to no one's regret. It causes us to pause and think

By Natalie J. Block

about the legacy each of us will leave behind.

So what did Jehoram do that was so terrible? Well, in short, he "did evil in the eyes of the LORD" (2 Chronicles 21:6) and led the people away from God (see 2 Chronicles 21:11). Jehoram was a powerful man who used his influence to leave a legacy of evil.

In contrast, Dorcas (aka Tabitha) was a woman who left a legacy of love. She was a kind woman who was "always doing good and helping the poor" (Acts 9:36). This woman was dearly loved. When she died, everyone was filled with regret. They had lost someone who had made an impact on their lives, and they wondered how they would go on without her. Their grief was so profound that it apparently moved not only Peter's heart but God's heart as well, and Dorcas was raised from the dead!

What we do with our lives is important. How we spend our time, the priorities we set, the attitudes we project, the goals we achieve—even the things we neglect—say something about us. God has placed within mothers and grandmothers a desire to reach out to those in need—to "mother" not only our own sons, daughters, and grandchildren but also others outside our immediate families. Be a mother or grandmother to someone today. Open your heart. Change a life. Change the world.

A Prayer for You

Dear Father, open my heart not only to my own children and grandchildren but also to those outside my immediate family. Help me to live my life in a way that pleases you and brings joy to those around me. I want to be remembered with love. Amen.

A Prayer for Your Grandchild
FOCUS: Spiritual Growth

Dear Lord, today I pray for my grandchild's spiritual growth. I ask that you instill in him the desire to read and memorize your Word. Give him a passion to be in conversation with you. May loving and serving you be part of his daily life. I ask that you stay close to him and lead him to be transformed to your likeness, to reflect your grace, and to radiate your love. I pray this in Jesus's name, amen.

Knocking at the Door

"Look! I stand at the door and knock.
If you hear my voice and open the door,
I will come in, and we will share
a meal together as friends."
—REVELATION 3:20 (NLT)

At ten years of age, I meticulously memorized a number of special Bible chapters for a contest at my Sunday school. At the end of the year, I was excited to be rewarded with the gift of a beautiful silver tinplate picture of Jesus standing and knocking at the door. It was always on my bedroom wall while I was growing up, and I treasure it even today.

With pleasure I enjoy sharing with my grandchildren the significance of Jesus standing and knocking at our heart's door. He wants to be invited in to forgive our sin and be our forever friend in fun and fellowship.

By Margaret Fishback Powers

Jesus will not push the door open, however, just as my grandchildren would never push the door to my bedroom open. Instead, they continually and patiently knock until I open the door and answer them. Jesus does the same. He keeps knocking, but He wants our hearts today!

My grandkids love to play a game on Saturday mornings by knocking gently on my door. They knock with a certain musical rhythm to see if I can guess which one of them it is. I laugh and make up various guesses, like

Tinker Bell, the tooth fairy, etc., even though I know each of their voices.

Jesus is knocking at our heart's door, asking us to open our lives to Him. He knows our voice and is waiting for us to respond. Children everywhere have faith to understand this illustration of love. They are always thrilled to receive one of my tiny pictures of Jesus at the door as a gift that I hand out when I am traveling.

Jesus is knocking. Open the door of your heart and welcome Him in.

A Prayer for You

O Jesus, our forever friend, I pray for your children, those of all ages and of all places. Open their ears that they will hear your knock and your voice calling them. Open their hearts that they will welcome you into their lives. Amen.

A Prayer for Your Grandchild
FOCUS: Salvation

Dear Lord, please guide my grandchild to your gift of salvation. I pray that she will come to know you, to love you, and to walk close to you throughout her life. May she boldly claim Jesus as her Lord and Savior. Guide her as she makes choices that have eternal consequences. Help her to follow you each moment of her life. I pray this in Jesus's name, amen.

day 45

Practicing Self-Discipline

*Apply your heart to instruction
and your ears to words of knowledge.*
—PROVERBS 23:12

God's Word instructs us as parents and grandparents to train our little ones in the way they should go (see Proverbs 22:6). Through our example and guidance, they will learn to speak kindly to all and accept discipline from their elders.

My granddaughter Lianna went through a sarcastic phase during which she would correct simple statements I made. Her mother, Kristy, would tell her to say she was sorry. Sometimes Lianna would apologize to me; other times she would stand defiantly, hands on her hips and lower lip curled under. "I'm not sorry," she would say. When she refused to apologize, her mother would say softly, "You need to take a time-out until you can come back and be pleasant."

Lianna learned quite quickly that her mother meant business, so she would slink off to the dining room and climb up into an armchair.

By Florence Littauer

Sometimes she would sit there quietly for fifteen minutes, hands folded and lower lip curled. Finally she would walk out to her mother, put her arms around her mother's knees, and say, "I'm sorry." This discipline worked well, and she learned not to correct me or anyone else.

One day I was visiting, and I looked down the hall toward Lianna's room. She was standing against the wall with her face leaning into her folded hands. I beckoned to Kristy to take a look and whispered, "What is she doing?"

Kristy smiled and said, "She's done something wrong, and she's giving herself a time-out before I discover what she did."

What a great idea—to punish yourself before someone catches you. If you can teach that to a child at four years old, you will save yourself and your little ones a lot of trouble in the future. So much of discipline can work in both directions as we all try to do what pleases the Lord.

A Prayer for You

Dear Lord Jesus, thank you for this lesson from a little child. Lord, let me see the error of my ways, accept the blame, confess to you, and continue to improve my relationships with others. Forgive me for the mistakes I've made. Pour your love upon me. In the name of the Lord, amen.

A Prayer for Your Grandchild
FOCUS: Emotional Development

O God, Creator of mind and body, I pray that you will give my grandchild emotional health and strength. Where there is anger, bring peace. Where there is confusion, bring clarity and focus. Where there are dark shadows, cast a ray of hope. Fill her with the sunshine of your Spirit. Warm her with the presence of your peace. In Jesus's name, amen.

day 46

A Moment to Shine

*"Whoever welcomes one such child
in my name welcomes me."*
—MATTHEW 18:5

My life has not been what you would call "normal." But my grandkids have never noticed. They've always thought all grandmothers were like "GranDot." Didn't all grandmas wear beaded gowns, ride tour buses, and sing on television? They seemed to think so.

Loving my grandbabies like I do, I have always enjoyed showing them off—giving them a chance to sparkle and shine. So I decided to take them *By Dottie Rambo* along to one of my concerts. I had the perfect song for them: "Germs," a song about an invisible dog that my grandson, Israel, loved singing.

So the night came. My two grandchildren, Destiny, age five, and Israel, age three, were led on stage. As I introduced the song—telling about its place on my children's record—I failed to notice that Israel had been drawn to the glint of my guitar's tuning keys.

While I chatted away, he started turning each shiny chrome tuner. The audience laughed and shouted, but I thought they were just being lively. That is, until I tried to start the song! When I hit what was supposed to be the first chord, my low E string fell off. I looked to Igs and

Des, who were both giggling. I looked at the audience, who were now roaring with laughter, and I started laughing myself. There's nothing like a spontaneous moment between you, your grandkids, and a few thousand of your closest friends!

God's the same way. He sets you up to sparkle and shine. And if you somehow untune everything your first time out, He'll just smile and laugh because He loves you.

A Prayer for You

Heavenly Father, thank you for the times we get to spend with our grandchildren. May each moment shimmer and shine in the glow of your love. In Jesus's precious name, amen.

A Prayer for Your Grandchild
FOCUS: Self-Image

O loving God, I praise you for creating my grandchild as a special, unique individual. Now I ask you to help him appreciate his uniqueness. Build up his self-image so he can enjoy his individuality. Help him to stand for who he is, where he has come from, and what he believes in. Encourage him not only to have hopes and dreams for the future but also to enjoy each day as it comes. In Jesus's name, amen.

day 47

Pray Like Daniel

Now when Daniel learned that the decree had been published, he went home to his upstairs room where the windows opened toward Jerusalem. Three times a day he got down on his knees and prayed, giving thanks to his God, just as he had done before.
—DANIEL 6:10

A phone call from Oma (our German grandmother) brought discouraging news: "Because of my eye problems and my knee surgery, the doctor won't let me travel anymore," she said. "I can't fly out to see you next month. In fact I can't do much of anything. Certainly can't sew or bake like I once did. I just sit around with my leg elevated, totally useless!"

The next evening Oma phoned again. "God showed me something special I can do every day—in fact, three times a day," she said cheerfully. "I can pray like Daniel—morning, noon, and night. So I've made a commitment to pray for all of you three times each day."

By Helen Haidle

Until the day she died five years later, Oma faithfully continued her "Daniel prayers." She knew it was her "work," an assignment from God.

Before getting out of bed each morning, she praised God, then she prayed for her family and others in need. Specific prayers were said for each child and grandchild.

She included her eight brothers and sisters, their children and grandchildren—praying for each one by name.

After lunch she would read her worn Bible and pray once more. At night, she prayed again.

"I'm praying down three generations," she explained. "My mother did this for her children, grandchildren, and great-grandchildren. Now I'm doing the same. I hope you will too," she added. "Remember how Lois handed her faith down to Eunice and also to Timothy." (See 2 Timothy 1:5.)

Many people learned to value Oma's daily prayers. After her funeral, we all asked each other, "Who will pray for us now?"

When I left the gravesite, a new thought comforted me: Her prayers still surround us and will continue to bless us.

A Prayer for You

Thank you, dear Lord, for the privilege of intercession. You've promised to hear my prayers and answer them. Help me to never grow weary as I intercede for my family and for those in need—three times a day and three generations down. Amen.

A Prayer for Your Grandchild
FOCUS: Prayer

Gracious Father, thank you for the avenue of prayer. Holy Spirit, please instill within the heart of my grandchild the desire to talk with you in prayer—to be open and transparent with you and to trust you enough to share her cares, prayers, and concerns.

Loving the Extra Child

When the LORD began to speak through Hosea, the LORD said to him, "Go marry a promiscuous woman and have children with her, for like an adulterous wife this land is guilty of unfaithfulness to the LORD."
—HOSEA 1:2

God instructed Hosea to do the seemingly impossible: accept and love an adulterous woman as his wife, and accept her children. The first child was Hosea's (see Hosea 1:3). Who fathered the other two is questionable (see Hosea 1:6, 8).

Many of us have a similar challenge in accepting and nurturing "grandchildren" who are not related to us either genetically or legally.

Who are these children to us? How should we care for them? God answers this question for us. All children are God's children, and Jesus reminds us to welcome them: "Whoever welcomes one of these little children in my name welcomes me" (Mark 9:37).

I have an "additional" grandchild. My daughter deserted her three children, leaving them with her husband. He also has a son by another relationship. Although I am fortunate to still see my grandchildren regularly, I struggle with my feelings for him. How can I love him in the same way or similarly to how I love my daughter's children?

By Donna Huisjen

My head may not be able to figure it all out, but my heart can overcome it. All children need love, acceptance, and attention. Everyone wants to belong to a family. The psalmist reminds us that "God sets the lonely in families" (Psalm 68:6). I've learned this: like the word *neighbor* in Luke 10:25–37, *family* is a fluid term in God's vocabulary. As Christians we can love all our grandchildren with God's help. We have been instructed: "Since God so loved us, we also ought to love one another" (1 John 4:11).

With God's grace, I can show love. Perhaps by continually expressing actions of love to each of the "additional" grandchildren who come into my life, my heart will be unable to distinguish among them.

A Prayer for You

Creator of all, you who knits together each child in his or her mother's womb, help me to embrace each little one in my extended family with equal enthusiasm and commitment. Help me to show them your love shining through me. Amen.

A Prayer for Your Grandchild
FOCUS: Respect for Authority

Dear Lord, I pray that my grandchild will continually grow to respect those in authority. May she learn to be cooperative and fair in work and play. Instill in her a high regard for officials who govern our land and enforce the laws. May her relationships with parents, teachers, coaches, mentors, and bosses be respectful, admirable, constructive, and caring. Amen.

day 49

Let It Go!

Then he fell on his knees and cried out,
"Lord, do not hold this sin against them."
When he had said this, he fell asleep.
—ACTS 7:60

I was the fifth generation living in the 1940s: my mother, her mother, my mother's father's mother, and her mother. Three generations lived in the same back-alley apartment in Dallas. I was raised by my great-grandmother, Sarah Harrell, who cared for her mother, my Grandma Molly, in that home.

I remember Grandma Molly as clearly today as I did sixty years ago. Her smooth black skin that had no wrinkles reminded me of someone who had oiled themselves with baby oil. Her tall, stately, erect posture and the twist on the back of her head rendered her sophisticated and royal. I watched her take her hair down at night and brush her long, silky black hair until it flowed like the mane of a well-kept stallion. Everything was right about Grandma Molly but one thing: she dipped snuff.

By Thelma Wells

One day I heard an awful yell. Angry words bellowed from downstairs in the flower garden. It was my great-grandmother screaming at the top of her lungs, "Mama, didn't you see me down here? You spit that snuff in the middle of my head! Don't you ever do that again! You look before you spit!" Sarah's tirade continued.

114

Daddy Harrell had to come to Grandma Molly's rescue and exclaimed, "Sweetie, that's enough. Molly feels bad enough; she didn't see you. She would not deliberately spit on you. Now, cut that noise out!" It was quite an argument.

Have you ever been hurt by someone who loves you? Whether they intended the harm or not, cut out that noise in your mind and heart, and let it go. Be inspired by Stephen, who reacted mercifully rather than vengefully toward those who were stoning him for his beliefs and convictions.

A Prayer for You

Understanding Father, when my feelings get hurt and I feel spit upon, please give me the mind and heart to forgive and let the hurt go. In Jesus's name, amen.

A Prayer for Your Grandchild
FOCUS: Character

Dear Lord and Father, I ask that you fill my grandchild with your Spirit so his character reflects your goodness and love. Give him kindness and love for others. Bring joy to his life so he will be a joy to others. Grant him patience and self-control through difficult and trying times. May he show mercy and generosity to those who are less fortunate. Grant him integrity and a sense of justice, and surround him with your peace. Amen.

day 50

Saying Grace, Singing Thanks

So whether you eat
or drink or whatever you do,
do it all for the glory of God.
—1 CORINTHIANS 10:31

When I was a young girl, frequent visits to my grandparents' farm gave me a wonderful connection to the earth and its bounty. I can still feel the warmth of the egg my grandmother pulled out from beneath her "laying hen" in the chicken house, and I can still taste the sweetness of the yellow corn steaming on my plate shortly after it was picked from the cornfield. Today we get these things from grocery stores, where the display of fruits and vegetables is endless and the connection to the earth and the hand of God that provided the rain and soil can be easily overlooked.

I am thankful for grandparents, who openly thanked God for His bounty at every meal, no matter how sparse or grand it was. A simple "Thank you for your provisions, Lord" was automatic.

By Bobbie Wolgemuth

These days, one of my favorite mealtime songs when our grandchildren visit is the doxology. Joining our voices around the table to sing "Praise God from whom all blessings flow . . ." is a familiar reminder that all we have—our health, our food, our family, our every breath—is a gift from our heavenly Father's hand. As a grandmother, I want to model gratefulness for the provisions He has made for our health.

Saying grace at meals is a family ritual that binds our hearts together in appreciation for God's goodness. It is extra fun to hold hands around the table for the blessing. Let the children join to sing or say their thanks to God at mealtime.

A Prayer for You

Lord Jesus, today I am thankful for all you have provided. Help me to show my grandchildren a grateful heart so they may enter the special blessing of noticing your abundance in the small and grand gifts you bestow on us every day. Amen.

A Prayer for Your Grandchild
FOCUS: Relationships at Home

O Lord, I pray that you will bless the home and family of my grandchild. May the relationships he has with his parents and siblings enhance his well-being, support his self-confidence, and increase his faith. May his home life reflect your love, your grace, your compassion, and your peace. Guide his parents to direct him in love and truth, so he will grow into a strong and compassionate individual. Amen.

day 51

A Model of Christ's Love

And now, dear lady,
I am not writing you a new command
but one we have had from the beginning.
I ask that we love one another.
—2 JOHN 5

It is not easy to love the way Jesus loved. His love was marked by sacrifice and suffering, a love that gave without limits. And this is the type of love He calls us to have for each other (see John 13:34–35). As I came to have a stronger relationship with Jesus, I began to consider this love—this giving, selfless love, and I realized it was being demonstrated in my life from my very own mother. My mom's activities were always geared around showing love for my four siblings and me, and for our dad—who struggled with health issues for decades. My mom worked tirelessly to help our family: She cooked for us, cleaned for us, and worked behind the scenes so our family would be happy and whole.

By Karen Kingsbury

But not until I had kids of my own did I really understand my mother's unconditional love. I realized then that my siblings and I had at times acted in ways that must have disappointed her. Yet I never felt her love waiver—not for me or my siblings. Not ever. So I've looked to her way of loving as an example of how I should, in turn, love my children.

The best part is this: Now I get the privilege of watching my mother love my kids the same way she has always loved me and my siblings. She is supportive of her grandkids if they are failing in math or struggling with health or are in the limelight finding great success.

I am grateful that God gave me a mother who not only raised me right but who also modeled the sort of love I, in turn, need to show my children and grandchildren. It's a love that Christ taught us—a love that He commanded we show one another.

A Prayer for You

Dear Lord, help me to look to those around me who have portrayed your love so clearly. Thank you for godly mothers, who are examples to all of us. And thank you for being the first one to show us what love really means. In Jesus's name, amen.

A Prayer for Your Grandchild
FOCUS: Spiritual Growth

Dear Lord, today I pray for my grandchild's spiritual growth. I ask that you instill in him the desire to read and memorize your Word. Give him a passion to be in conversation with you. May loving and serving you be part of his daily life. I ask that you stay close to him and lead him to be transformed to your likeness, to reflect your grace, and to radiate your love. I pray this in Jesus's name, amen.

day 52

"Honey, You're Doing So Well"

I will boast all the more gladly about my
weaknesses, so that Christ's power may rest on me.
That is why, for Christ's sake, I delight in weaknesses,
in insults, in hardships, in persecutions, in difficulties.
For when I am weak, then I am strong.
—2 CORINTHIANS 12:9–10

One evening, my three grandchildren were bowed in absorbed earnestness, fitting colored beads onto a framed template. Reading nearby, I heard Josie (age nine) say to her cousin Elias (age six), "Oh, honey, you're doing so well." How cute, I thought. She's three years older, but to her, Elias is still "honey."

Next I heard Josie say to her brother Ayden (age five), "Good job. You really are making a wonderful picture."

We all need words of praise to keep us going, no matter what our age. I have numbers dyslexia that leaves me vulnerable to the accusation by certain family members that I am "detail ditzy." I will not bore you with descriptions of my lifetime of misadventures,

By Karen Mains

but one time, on the day before flying out of town, I noticed that the tickets I booked to visit my son's family in Phoenix left Chicago's O'Hare International Airport at 9:00 p.m. (not a.m.) on February 17. This meant that I would arrive the next day, February 18, at 12:30 a.m. instead of at 12:30 p.m. on February 17, as I had thought.

What I am learning is this: My inadequacies are an opportunity for God's adequacies. That lost Friday, for example, when I was supposed to arrive in Phoenix around noon but arrived around midnight—well, I really, really needed that whole day to finish up a pile of work I didn't know I would have to finish.

When God looks at my life, He says, "Honey, you're doing so well." He knows about my brain-glitch thingy (keys left in the ignition of running parked cars, etc.), and He doesn't get frustrated, distressed, irritated, or bent out of sorts with me. Instead, He says, "Let me show you what I can do with these inadequacies of yours." So, I am attempting to apply His (and my granddaughter's) salve to my own inward and frequent frustration: "Honey . . ."

A Prayer for You

Lord, it is hard to love myself—flaws and all. So instead, help me to take delight in the sometimes funny, but always intriguing, ways you use my weaknesses to bring me to the realization (again and again) that I am going to always be dependent upon your strength. Amen.

A Prayer for Your Grandchild
FOCUS: Courage

O Father, builder of character and courage, may my grandchild grow strong in the light of your face. Grant him courage to stand for what is right, to guard the truth, and to ensure justice in every aspect of life. May he boldly grow in grace, revere your name, and proudly proclaim you as the Lord of Lords and King of Kings.

day 53

Keeping the Peace

Make every effort to keep the unity
of the Spirit through the bond of peace.
—EPHESIANS 4:3

As we left our son's house the day they brought their first child home from the hospital, my husband asked, "Can we trust mere parents to raise our grandson?"

As a grandmother, I'm learning how hard that can be. After all my years of parenting experience, why do they want to do things *their* way instead of asking me how to do them? Then I remember how my mother-in-law objected to putting "that poor little baby" in a car seat every trip. That was the closest she and I ever came to quarreling. I insisted because *I* was the mother. Eventually she reluctantly consented.

It is tragic when differences of opinion in a family escalate into quarrels that estrange grandparents from their adult children and precious grandchildren. That's why we grandmothers need to remember Paul's exhortation to make *every effort* to preserve unity through the bond of peace. In relating to our children who are also parents, "every effort" may include swallowing our advice—and our pride. It includes praise when our children "parent" better than we did. It includes searching hard for a tactful way to put forth an alternative

By Patricia Sprinkle

suggestion. And when discussions get heated? I once heard: "Always apologize. If you are right, you can afford to. If you are wrong, you can't afford not to."

Staying connected to our grandchildren's lives is well worth the price.

A Prayer for You

Lord, remind me that my adult children do not need my advice as much as they need my love and support while they seek to parent their own children. Amen.

A Prayer for Your Grandchild
FOCUS: Emotional Development

O God, Creator of mind and body, I pray that you will give my grandchild emotional health and strength. Where there is anger, bring peace. Where there is confusion, bring clarity and focus. Where there are dark shadows, cast a ray of hope. Fill her with the sunshine of your Spirit. Warm her with the presence of your peace. In Jesus's name, amen.

day 54

In the Storm

He stilled the storm to a whisper,
the waves of the sea were hushed.
—PSALM 107:29

It was a cloudy day in Dallas. Storms were in the forecast, but my oldest daughter needed to be transported from a retreat site in East Texas to Dallas. So my two young granddaughters, their godmother, and I embarked on a road trip on a sunny afternoon to pick her up. Beautiful scenery and playing games in the car made it delightful.

My daughter was waiting for us. Immediately, we started our return journey home to Dallas. Within a few minutes I noticed dark clouds on the horizon. I became suspicious of the developing ominous clouds, wondering if there was a funnel, indicating a tornado.

By Sheila Bailey

Suddenly a torrential rain began to fall. We were in a storm!

Sirens were alarming our phones. Nervousness heightened as I drove through Canton. One granddaughter said, "It is time to go to sleep," and she cuddled her entire body under the blanket. Her younger sister was ready for a science lesson as she asked one question after another. I didn't have a weather app or an operable radio station so we would know what was ahead.

So we prayed. We asked the Lord for safety, calmness, and wisdom.

Finally, after what seemed like a long time, we experienced God calming the storm. By God's amazing grace we arrived home safely, only to learn that Canton had been hit—and there was destruction and death because of the storm. We prayed for the people of that city—and we thanked God for protecting us.

"Through many dangers, toils and snares I have already come," wrote the writer of "Amazing Grace." And indeed it is God's "grace that leads us home."

A Prayer for You

Thank you God, for taking us through the storm. Allow my testimonies of how you have answered my prayers throughout life to encourage my grandchildren to trust you more. Amen.

A Prayer for Your Grandchild
FOCUS: Prayer

Dear heavenly Father, may my grandchild love you more and know more clearly that you love her. Teach her to speak to you and listen to you in prayer. Give her a heart that trusts you to calm the difficulties she faces, because you are the One who calms the storms of life.

Jael's Story

"Most blessed of women be Jael,
the wife of Heber the Kenite,
most blessed of tent-dwelling women."
—JUDGES 5:24

Everyone has family stories. Imagine the stories Jael's children recounted about *their* mother. Her legendary actions were heralded in song by another renowned woman: Deborah (see Judges 5:24–27). Jael was a heroine among the Israelites, and the people applauded her bravery.

Jael's story is often overlooked when we recount Bible stories. We tend to pass over the first stories in Judges—heading straight to Gideon (Judges 6) and then leaping to Samson (Judges 13). We make no mention of Deborah and her amazing leadership, of Barak the warrior, or of Jael's grisly slaying of Sisera, the enemy of Israel. Perhaps the story is just too gory. Perhaps we cringe at the thought of Jael's cunning and trickery. We don't like the thought of a woman plotting an assassination. The imagery is disconcerting: a hammer, a tent peg, a sleeping man—yikes! Let's not tell this one to the grandkids.

By Doris Wynbeek Rikkers

Yet Jael's children and grandchildren must have loved retelling the story of their mom and grandma to others. Though Jael's husband, Heber the Kenite, apparently had allied himself with Israel's enemies (see Judges 4:11, 17),

Jael remained true to the Kenites' longstanding alliance with Israel. When the Israelites were threatened, Jael did not stand idly by. When she had the opportunity to act, she acted. The results of that fateful day, culminated by Jael's bravery, were significant: "Then the land had peace forty years" (Judges 5:31).

Nevertheless, it is difficult in our culture and within our peace-loving minds to praise the bloody acts recounted in the Bible. We are horrified by the wars and bloodshed. But these are the kinds of stories that the Israelites were commanded to retell to their children. It was their duty to pass on the history of their nation and to applaud the brave acts of those who kept their nation intact and protected from outside forces that wished to destroy Israel.

Few of us will ever become legends or be heralded in song like Jael was, but all of us have stories. All of us will be remembered in family stories (or legends) or family histories for some characteristic or special act or event. What stories will your children and grandchildren tell about you?

A Prayer for You

Dear Lord and Father, thank you for using ordinary men and women to further your plans and establish your kingdom. Help me to be brave and discerning, like Jael, and to know your will and act upon it. Amen.

A Prayer for Your Grandchild
FOCUS: Courage

O Father, builder of character and courage, may my grandchild grow strong in the light of your face. Grant him courage to stand for what is right, to guard the truth, and to ensure justice in every aspect of life. May he boldly grow in grace, revere your name, and proudly proclaim you as the Lord of Lords and King of Kings.

day 56

Fruity Folks

The fruit of the Spirit is love, joy, peace, forbearance, kindness, goodness, faithfulness, gentleness and self-control.
—GALATIANS 5:22–23

We tend to think two crazy truths about the fruit of the Spirit: First, we think that the fruit of the Spirit is all about being nice, nice, nice all the time. Visions of "Church Lady" come into our thinking. (I wonder why, since she was not really all that nice.) The fruit of the Spirit is *not* about being nice. It's about being like Jesus.

Jesus was always filled with the fruit of the Spirit. But He wasn't always nice. When He told the Pharisees to stop making faith harder than God makes it, that wasn't nice. Or when He told the woman caught in adultery to stop sinning, that wasn't nice. Or when He drove *By Elisa Morgan* the money-changers out of the temple, that wasn't nice. Jesus wasn't always nice. But He was always filled with the Spirit.

Second, we think that it is all up to us to grow the fruit of the Spirit. We think that if we try hard enough, we'll evidence these qualities. This will never happen! No matter how much we strain and stretch, we cannot grow such attributes in our lives. The fruit of the Spirit is just that: God's character reproduced by His power in our lives. These traits are up to *Him* to grow, not us.

The fruit of the Spirit represent the qualities we possess when we look like God.

A Prayer for You

Dear plant-growing God, please cultivate in me your character qualities. I yield to you to reproduce in me the traits that come from your nature. Let these characteristics be evidence to this world of your love so those who are truly hungry will find a relationship with you. Amen.

A Prayer for Your Grandchild
FOCUS: Spiritual Growth

Dear Lord, today I pray for my grandchild's spiritual growth. I ask that you instill in him the desire to read and memorize your Word. Give him a passion to be in conversation with you. May loving and serving you be part of his daily life. I ask that you stay close to him and lead him to be transformed to your likeness, to reflect your grace, and to radiate your love. I pray this in Jesus's name, amen.

day 57

Let Me Tell You about My Grandchildren (1)

There is a time for everything, . . .
a time to be silent and a time to speak.
—ECCLESIASTES 3:1, 7

"Let me tell you about my grandchildren" is *not* music to some people's ears. Despite the fact that baby pictures are adorable and that sweet children's antics are amusing, not everyone wants to hear about your grandchildren! Can you imagine?

A grandmother's understanding of the appropriate moment to pull out the pictures or to tell the cute story is something we all need to keep in mind. *Sensitivity is the key.* Remember to whom you are speaking and remember what her level of interest might be in your descendants. Those two factors determine what to tell and how much to tell.

If you are speaking to another grandmother who has lavished her stories on you, then go for it. Tell your stories and show your pictures to your heart's content. If, however, you are talking with someone who may not *By Jan Silvious* have grandchildren or someone who may have suffered a loss, remember to be tender and appropriate.

I have a sweet friend who has lost several unborn grandbabies through her daughter's miscarriages. To date, there is not a living grandchild in her life. Although she often asks about my grandchildren, out of deference to her, I reference them with general statements and quickly change the subject.

I would love to see the day when we could delight in one another's grandchildren and all the joy they bring. Until then, I want to love her with the gift of appropriate restraint. That is something we can do for one another as we live as friends. Being sensitive and being appropriate keeps relationships intact. Sometimes, our personal elation blinds us to the hurts in another's life.

A Prayer for You

Father, make me a sensitive friend. Tug on my spirit with a call for restraint if I ever step over the line of what is gracious and appropriate. Give me eyes to see beyond what I think and open my heart to hear what you would have me say and do. Amen.

A Prayer for Your Grandchild
FOCUS: Respect for Authority

Dear Lord, I pray that my grandchild will continually grow to respect those in authority. May he learn to be cooperative and fair in work and play. Instill in him a high regard for officials who govern our land and enforce the laws. May his relationships with parents, teachers, coaches, mentors, and bosses be respectful, admirable, constructive, and caring. Amen.

day 58

Let Me Tell You about My Grandchildren (2)

Love is patient, love is kind.
It does not envy, it does not boast, it is not proud.
It does not dishonor others, it is not self-seeking.
—1 CORINTHIANS 13:4–5

For an hour and a half I listened to an acquaintance recount the sterling accomplishments of her children. She was justly proud, but her boasting devoured our lunch and left me feeling left out of the conversation and left out as a mother of high achievers. As I examined my feelings, I remembered Paul's description of the qualities of love that I needed to exercise at this time: patience, kindness, and selflessness.

By Cynthia Heald

I also became aware of the importance of being considerate of others when I converse with them. The Scriptures are clear that if I am to be a woman who loves, I do not boast. To *boast* means to "vaunt or extol the deeds or abilities of oneself or of another; to flaunt; to sing one's own praises." It is good and right to share stories about our families, but we cross the line of love when we become so absorbed with ourselves that we become insensitive to others.

I heard the story of a woman who had just been with her first grandchild. When this new grandmother saw a friend having lunch with a young couple in a restaurant, she rushed over to her friend and excitedly began showing pictures and sharing how cute and healthy the baby was. After she left, the couple no longer wanted to eat or talk, for they had just lost their newborn baby two weeks before. Certainly this grandmother did not know about the couple's loss, but if she had been committed to not boasting, perhaps her intrusion would not have caused such pain.

One privilege of being a grandmother is sharing how special our grandchildren are, but let us share with humility and thoughtfulness—for love does not boast.

A Prayer for You

O Father, how easy it is to talk about "me." May I be more concerned about the interests of others than I am about my own interests. Set a guard over my lips so that boasting is restrained and replaced by love. Amen.

A Prayer for Your Grandchild
FOCUS: Spiritual Growth

Dear Lord, today I pray for my grandchild's spiritual growth. I ask that you instill in her the desire to read and memorize your Word. Give her a passion to be in conversation with you. May loving and serving you be part of her daily life. I ask that you stay close to her and lead her to be transformed to your likeness, to reflect your grace, and to radiate your love. I pray this in Jesus's name, amen.

day 59

The Hand Goes Up

The LORD is good, a refuge in times of trouble.
He cares for those who trust in him.
—NAHUM 1:7

As Maggie, my toddler granddaughter, was circling the backyard, she was drawn to a specific pathway. A sharp, concrete patio corner lined one side and a heavy, potted cactus bordered the other. Tomorrow, Grandpa would have to remove the cactus from the backyard, but today the solution was to follow closely in my granddaughter's footsteps. As she approached the trail, I instructed, "Hold Grandma's hand, honey. I don't want you to fall and get hurt."

Each time she circled the yard and approached the hazardous pathway, Maggie automatically raised her hand up to me. She never checked to see if I was following her closely. She just lifted her hand high over her head with confidence, knowing that I would not let her fall.

If I could only be that trusting of God! As I approach a hazardous point in my life's pathway, how I wish that I would always have the complete trust to automatically put my hand up to Him. I know with confidence *By Cheryl Baker* that He is there; however, sometimes I try to take matters into my own hands. When I choose to rely only on myself, I usually fall and get hurt.

Although most of the book of Nahum contains words of prophetic judgment directed to Nineveh, the dreaded oppressor of Judah, the book was meant for the Israelites. Through Nahum, the Lord assured His people that "he cares for those who trust in him" (Nahum 1:7).

At the time of our backyard walk, I realized that my precious granddaughter was quickly approaching her two-year birthday. With that milestone, she would slip into the "I wanna do this by myself" stage. And for a time, she will stop automatically raising her hand up to those of us who want to protect her from falling. As her family, it is crucial that we teach her about the love of Christ and demonstrate our reliance on God's power to keep us from a fall.

A Prayer for You

Dear Lord and Father, thank you for your protection during the difficult times of my life. As my grandchildren grow up, I pray that when they approach hazardous turning points along their pathway, they will lift their hands with confidence toward you. Amen.

A Prayer for Your Grandchild
FOCUS: Salvation

Dear Lord, please guide my grandchild to your gift of salvation. I pray that she will come to know you, love you, and to walk close to you throughout her life. May she boldly claim Jesus as her Lord and Savior. Guide her as she makes choices that have eternal consequences. Help her to follow you each moment of her life. I pray this in Jesus's name, amen.

day 60

The Singing Grandma

*Miriam sang to them: "Sing to the LORD,
for he is highly exalted. Both horse and driver
he has hurled into the sea."*
—EXODUS 15:21

I sing almost all the time. My family is musical, and my husband and I record albums for kids and have led worship at our church. Songs bubble out of me as I come through the doors at work, drive in the car, or pick out melons at the market. My neighbors know I am in the store from *By Debby Kerner Rettino* the next aisle over. Praise songs, old hymns, or my latest composition—it is quite unconscious. I sing almost constantly, and it drives my grandson crazy. At thirteen years of age, it is soooo embarrassing to be out with Grandma. I try to curb my spontaneous melodies when I am in public with him. (Something about not provoking your children to wrath comes to mind.)

When he was little, I would sing into his ear, "Who loves you more than I do?" He would answer in his tiny, toddler voice, "God does." That's the best wisdom I could give him. Over and over and over I sang about God's love for him in his ear. I wanted it to stick. I wanted it to stick so that when he faced temptation, the songs I sang in his ear would come back to him. I wanted it to stick so that when he smacked into the realities of life, not only would he remember how much I loved him, but more important, God's love for him would also be engraved on his heart. I wanted it to stick so that when he faced hard things in his future, he would remember that his grandma loved him like crazy—but God loved him more.

So I sing. Almost all the time.

A Prayer for You

Father in heaven, thank you for the song you have put in my heart. I praise you for the Word of God that lives in me and bubbles over in music. Thank you that no matter how much I love my grandkids, you love them more than I do.

A Prayer for Your Grandchild
FOCUS: Worship

Dear Lord, you are worthy of worship. Please guide my grandchild to sense the value of worship, especially corporate worship with other believers in the body of Christ. Help him to know the value of meeting together at church with others who share a love for Jesus Christ, and help him to know that worshiping, learning from God's Word, and gaining insights from other believers at church are vital to his spiritual growth.

day 61

Perpetuating Memories

*I will perpetuate your memory through
all generations; therefore the nations
will praise you for ever and ever.*
—PSALM 45:17

What will your grandchild remember? Mine will probably always remember that "Momo broke de door."

At twenty months old, my grandson locked himself in his father's study. He was too young to turn the knob, so after rejecting several alternatives, I found a sturdy wrench and commanded, "Go stand near the window! I have to break down the door!"

He stood—frozen and wide-eyed—across the room, watching my disembodied hand coming through the jagged hole I had smashed so I could to reach the knob. For weeks afterwards, every time he passed that room, he'd announce, "Momo broke de door."

His parents and I decided to teach him an additional part of the story. When he'd say, "Momo broke de door," we'd ask, "Why did Momo break the door?" He'd beam as he repeated the answer we'd 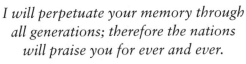 *By Patricia Sprinkle* taught him: "To save me." He knows he's worth saving!

Psalm 45 is a song in praise of Israel's king on his wedding day. In verse 17 the psalmist pledged to perpetuate the king's memory throughout the generations and awaken the praise of the nations.

One of the privileges of being a grandparent is passing on faith-building stories to future generations. My father told us how his father assembled his nine children nightly for family devotions. Recently my son said of his little boy, "It's such fun to see Joshua picking up on spiritual rhythms. He expects to pray before meals and bedtime. He knows to say 'Amen' after a prayer." Joshua has learned those rhythms through stories and memories from generations of believers. I suspect one of the earliest memories he'll pass down will be "When Momo Broke de Door—to Save Me."

A Prayer for You

Lord, thank you for those who believed in you in the past and passed that faith on to me. Help me to perpetuate both their faith and their memories of your faithfulness.

A Prayer for Your Grandchild
FOCUS: Relationships at Home

O Lord, I pray that you will bless the home and family of my grandchild. May the relationships he has with his parents and siblings enhance his well-being, support his self-confidence, and increase his faith. May his home life reflect your love, your grace, your compassion, and your peace. Guide his parents to direct him in love and truth, so he will grow into a strong and compassionate individual. Amen.

Grandma to the Rescue!

*I have no greater joy than to hear
that my children are walking in the truth.*
—3 JOHN 4

Years ago, when he was little, our son, Jason, spent a few days with his grandparents in northern Michigan. One morning Grandpa helped prepare breakfast. Opening a jar of canned prunes, he filled three bowls with the wrinkled fruit and covered them with the juice. A few minutes later the three of them joined hands and Grandpa asked the *By Carol Kent* blessing. Grandma had prepared eggs, sausage, and toast. And there sat the prunes—lots of prunes.

Jason finished his breakfast but hadn't touched the prunes. Grandpa observed his reluctance to eat the squishy fruit and announced, "Jason, if you want to keep your 'plumbing' working properly, you'll have to eat your prunes, son."

Jason had always been an obedient child, but the smell of prunes made his stomach rumble. Amid gags and gulps, he finally managed to swallow all of the prunes.

Grandpa spoke, "Jason, the juice is just as good for you as the prunes, so why don't you empty that bowl, son?"

Jason gazed up at his grandma with desperation. Suddenly, Grandma said, "Clyde (that was Grandpa), I forgot to get the chicken out of the freezer in time to thaw for tonight's supper. Would you go downstairs and take care of that?"

While Grandpa headed to the basement, Grandma picked up Jason's prune juice and dumped it down the drain. Moving fast, she placed the bowl back on the table.

Grandpa returned, chicken in hand. Peering at Jason's empty bowl, he asked, "Now that wasn't so bad after all, was it?"

Jason's eyes locked with Grandma's, and they shared a moment of relief and humor before admitting what really had happened. It was a day that bonded Jason and Grandma—and they spent many future visits talking about biblical truths while weaving joyful memories into their precious times together.

A Prayer for You

Father, my earnest desire is to pass truth on to the next generation. Help me to remember that children learn best when they have a healthy balance of laughter and joy while they are learning. Amen.

A Prayer for Your Grandchild
FOCUS: Emotional Development

O God, Creator of mind and body, I pray that you will give my grandchild emotional health and strength. Where there is anger, bring peace. Where there is confusion, bring clarity and focus. Where there are dark shadows, cast a ray of hope. Fill her with the sunshine of your Spirit. Warm her with the presence of your peace. In Jesus's name, amen.

day 63

Mimi's Quilt

Very early in the morning, while it was still dark, Jesus got up, left the house and went off to a solitary place, where he prayed.
—MARK 1:35

Mimi was a grandmother from Pennsylvania farm country who was a powerhouse of prayer. She made gorgeous quilts with hand stitches so tiny that patterned works of art burst forth from the fabric. Mimi spent her early mornings kneeling in prayer next to a small bed draped with one of her handmade quilts. With her elbows up on the edge of the quilt, she prayed for her children and grandchildren, for missionaries, for churches, for the neighbors, for world events, for just about everything that the Lord Jesus brought to her mind as she knelt beside the bed every morning.

During the day, as she canned fruit, cooked, cleaned, or shopped, Mimi continued her prayer service for those who came to her mind. At age ninety-seven, Mimi died, and her family gathered her few simple belongings and set aside a quilt for each grandchild. There was one particular quilt that was the family's most prized possession. Not having one of the prettiest pat- *By Bobbie Wolgemuth* terns or colors, the treasured quilt was the one with two small spots on the edge where Mimi's elbows had worn into the fabric when she knelt to pray.

One of Mimi's granddaughters now has the prayer quilt, and the next generation will be told about the small woman who delighted in spending time on her knees before the throne of God.

What will your children and grandchildren treasure when you're gone? Maybe a prayer journal in which you've written their names and a verse you prayed for each child will be the most valuable thing you leave behind. Invest in time before the Father's throne today.

Rocking chairs, piano benches, and quilts can become places of prayer that carry your children and grandchildren to the place of blessing. Leave behind pieces of grace for every child.

A Prayer for You

Father in heaven, thank you for the privilege of prayer. Today remind me that you are the giver of gifts that last forever. Help me to invest in eternal things that will remind my grandchildren and great-grandchildren of your love and power. I want to give them the gift of prayer. Amen.

A Prayer for Your Grandchild
FOCUS: Character

Dear Lord and Father, I ask that you fill my grandchild with your Spirit so her character reflects your goodness and love. Give her kindness and love for others. Bring joy to her life so she will be a joy to others. Grant her patience and self-control through difficult and trying times. May she show mercy and generosity to those who are less fortunate. Grant her integrity and a sense of justice, and surround her with your peace. Amen.

day 64

Shine, Christian, Shine!

"No one lights a lamp and puts it in a place where it will be hidden, or under a bowl. Instead they put it on its stand, so that those who come in may see the light."

—LUKE 11:33

It is startling when the lights go out. You search for the candles and the match to light them. You think you're prepared with flashlights or lanterns, only to find that when the lights go out, you are scrambling to remember where you left them.

It seemed to be a calm thunderstorm and lightning show, nothing severe. But suddenly all the lights went out. It was pitch dark. My grandchildren were playing throughout the house. Darkness got their immediate attention.

They screamed, "Grammy, what happened? I can't see. Where are you? Come get me! Lights! Lights!" I tried to assure them that they were safe. I found a lighter and lit the candles throughout the house. The darkness was dispelled. The kids felt safer and started laughing about how scared they had been in the dark.

By Thelma Wells

I thought about the blackness, the darkness, the unrest of not being able to see anything clearly because there was no light. I recalled that sinning is an event of darkness in which a life is paralyzed by the inability to see things the way God sees them. Many people feel overcome by this darkness because they have nothing to illuminate their spirits. Sin engulfs people with questions similar to those of my grandchildren: "Help, where are you?" "Help, can you come get me?" "Where is the light? Lights, pleeease?"

As Christians we need to let our lights shine with the light of Jesus to illuminate the way and to help repel the darkness of sin. When we do, we will have the joy of a little child who feels safe when the lights return.

A Prayer for You

Jesus, may your light that lives in me be a beacon that is clear for people to see. I pray the same for my friends. In Jesus's name, amen.

A Prayer for Your Grandchild
FOCUS: Courage

O Father, builder of character and courage, may my grandchild grow strong in the light of your face. Grant him courage to stand for what is right, to guard the truth, and to ensure justice in every aspect of life. May he boldly grow in grace, revere your name, and proudly proclaim you as the Lord of Lords and King of Kings.

day 65

The Other Grandmother

Rejoice in the Lord always.
I will say it again: Rejoice!
—PHILIPPIANS 4:4

It had barely been twenty-four hours since my only grand-child—a cuddly eight-month-old girl—left my arms and home. Suddenly, a picture of her with her *other grandmother* showed up on my social media feed.

The way my granddaughter smiled at *her* was the same way she had smiled at me! The way her *other grandmother* held her—as if she was a very precious gift—was the same way I had held her just hours before!

My mind said, "They look so happy and I am happy for them." But my heart, my *heart* was saying something very different. My heart longed to be the one holding my granddaughter. Yes, she had just spent a full week with me, but it was not long enough. Yet a small voice within me kept saying, "Rejoice in the Lord always . . ." *Always.*

The other grandmother and I both live in Michigan, on opposite sides of the state. Our shared grandchild lives in California with her parents—my son and *her* daughter. Little

By Michelle R. Loyd-Paige

Miss Paxton is my first grandchild and the thirty-first grandchild for the other grandmother.

It is not easy being a long-distance grandmother. The desire to be closer is always present. I suspect that it is much like the desire our heavenly Father has for us to be closer to Him. How the Father's heart must ache when He sees us cast a loving gaze away from Him.

Although my heart aches, I am learning to rejoice that my granddaughter has *two loving grandmothers* and that we both get to spend time with her.

A Prayer for You

Heavenly Father, help my mind and heart rejoice when my granddaughter is with her other grandmother. Thank you for stretching my capacity to love and rejoice. Amen.

A Prayer for Your Grandchild
FOCUS: Prayer

Gracious Father, thank you for the avenue of prayer. Holy Spirit, please instill within the heart of my grandchild the desire to talk with you in prayer—to be open and transparent with you and to trust you enough to share his cares, prayers, and concerns. In Jesus's name, amen.

day 66

Overwhelming Love

Children's children are a crown to the aged,
and parents are the pride of their children.
—PROVERBS 17:6

Bitter cold accompanied our third grandson. Joshua Daniel Copeland threw us a curve ball on February 6, 1990. The typical excited phone call came, alerting the family of the imminent birth. Both sets of grandparents bundled up tightly and headed for the hospital, where we sat for several hours until our son Randy came out and told everyone to go home. The doctor said the birth wouldn't be until morning.

"Are you sure?" we questioned; we had been there for James's and Joe's births, and we didn't want to miss this one.

"Morning," Randy verified. "Go home and get some rest."

The anxious grandparents left, braving the cold wind and frosted windshields. We climbed wearily into bed around 1:00 a.m., and at 1:30 the phone rang. You guessed it. *By Lori Copeland* Randy was calling from the delivery room, where our third grandson had just decided to make his entrance. This child has never been a morning person.

Josh, the little blonde-headed boy who would clomp around in cowboy boots and hat, and manage to shoot a fly's eye out at thirty feet, entered our lives on "a slider." We now had three sons and three grandsons. We began planning for a baseball team.

In my early years, I wondered why God would send His Son to die on a cross for me—for anyone. Then I became a mother—and then a grandmother, and I realized with each birth the overwhelming love and protection I felt for both my children and my grandchildren. The "why" suddenly became clear: There is no stronger love than that of a parent or grandparent. Did God love His Son any less? When you pause to reflect on His sacrifice, His gift to humanity, you fall to your knees in humble gratitude and praise.

A Prayer for You

Father, you have blessed me with children and grandchildren. I don't know why. I don't question the reason. This I do know: You've given me these precious souls not because I'm worthy but because you are worthy, Lord. Amen.

A Prayer for Your Grandchild
FOCUS: Salvation

Dear Lord, please guide my grandchild to your gift of salvation. I pray that she will come to know you, to love you, and to walk close to you throughout her life. May she boldly claim Jesus as her Lord and Savior. Guide her as she makes choices that have eternal consequences. Help her to follow you each moment of her life. I pray this in Jesus's name, amen.

day 67

I Am Determined

Though the fig tree does not bud and there are
no grapes on the vines, though the olive crop fails and
the fields produce no food, though there are no sheep
in the pen and no cattle in the stalls, yet I will rejoice
in the LORD, I will be joyful in God my Savior.
—HABAKKUK 3:17–18

God showed the prophet Habakkuk that the powerful Babylonians were soon to destroy Judah. Yet Habakkuk concluded his book with an expression of faith—actually more than that: an expression of joy in the face of disaster that is one of the Bible's most incredible passages. Some might find it hard to keep faith when they stub a toe. Habakkuk was determined ("I will . . . I will") to keep faith when all seemed lost. The word *determined* is key here. Like Job (see Job 13:15), Habakkuk determined beforehand not to let his faith falter in the face of pain or tragedy.

I have known some rough times in my life. Illness and house fires are not small things. Through them all, my faith remained firm, no problem. But when my youngest granddaughter died suddenly, when I held my own daughter as she cried, "My baby, my *By Jean E. Syswerda* baby," my faith took a hit. How could I trust a God who would allow/permit/do/carry out (take your pick according to your theological inclination) such a horror, not just to us but also to her—three months old and so innocent? How could I follow a God who ruled a world with such sorrow in it? How could I even go on at all?

And that's where determination came into play. Like Habakkuk, I had to choose to rejoice. I had to choose to trust in God even when disaster hit and despair followed. Only two choices stood before me: I could turn away from God, or I could turn toward Him. As I considered those choices, I looked away and discovered complete and frightening nothingness. Then I looked toward God and decided that even if He provides no answers, even if more tragedy follows, even if the cloud never lifts from our lives, I will trust in Him. I will rejoice in Him. I am determined!

A Prayer for You

O Lord, what is the meaning of such suffering in life? Is there a purpose in it all? I've chosen to trust you, to believe that there is meaning and that you know what you are doing. I've decided that no matter what happens, I will rejoice in you, Lord; I will be joyful in God my Savior. Amen.

A Prayer for Your Grandchild
FOCUS: Relationships at Home

O Lord, I pray that you will bless the home and family of my grandchild. May the relationships she has with her parents and siblings enhance her well-being, support her self-confidence, and increase her faith. May her home life reflect your love, your grace, your compassion, and your peace. Guide her parents to direct her in love and truth, so she will grow into a strong and compassionate individual. Amen.

day 68

The Kindergarten Circus

The LORD your God is with you,
the Mighty Warrior who saves. He will take great
delight in you; in his love he will no longer rebuke
you, but will rejoice over you with singing.
—ZEPHANIAH 3:17

This is the season of my life when I attend events like the spring Kindergarten Circus for the morning class. My granddaughter, Joscelyn, was part of the elephant dance, the last act—after the tightrope walkers, the seals, the strong people, etc. Josie was dressed in what looked to be a very warm elephant outfit. She and her two partners had to sit in the front row under hot lights and wait a whole hour for their turn.

By Karen Mains

"Weren't you hot, Josie?" I asked after I had praised her for her remarkable two-step with the other elephant kindergartners. Pushing up her floppy elephant trunk, she shook her head up and down.

"I'm so sorry Papa couldn't come, but I'll tell him all about it."

"Oh, that's okay," she replied, "You were here, and that's what makes it so very special to me."

Coming home, I began to consider: Isn't much of life like the Kindergarten Circus? Everyone else comes first, doing their tumbling and fake weightlifting and rigged magic acts, and we're sitting in some conspicuous place wearing a hot, uncomfortable costume, waiting for our turn to do our little two-step. Then we realize that Someone is in the audience, Someone who has come just to watch us do whatever it is we do. We scoot around in our uncomfortable costume, but now it's okay.

God has come to be with us, to cheer and applaud, to wave from the audience, to say to our hearts, "I'm so very proud of you." None of the inconveniences really matter. Nor the fact that other people have been watching their children and don't care that we are hot and the wait has been long. God is present. That, indeed, is what makes everything so very special.

A Prayer for You

O Lord, help us to remember that when life begins to seem futile, you are always watching us—watching us with the unstinting favor of a proud and delighted grandparent. Amen.

A Prayer for Your Grandchild
FOCUS: Self-Image

O loving God, I praise you for creating my grandchild as a special, unique individual. Now I ask you to help her appreciate her uniqueness. Build up her self-image so she can enjoy her individuality. Help her to stand for who she is, where she has come from, and what she believes in. Encourage her not only to have hopes and dreams for the future but also to enjoy each day as it comes. In Jesus's name, amen.

day 69

Dawn

*Be still before the LORD
and wait patiently for him.*
—PSALM 37:7

I awakened early and got up to take a walk on the beach. But when I looked out, it was still dark. I sat down on the porch to wait for the sun to come up. I sat there for a bit with no hint of dawn. I poured myself a cup of coffee and returned to the porch to wait. It was quiet and still. Nothing seemed to be moving.

As I sat there, I saw the morning star . . . and the very faintest hint of light beginning in the horizon. Ever so slowly, the dawn crept up from the East. A lonely gull called, and through the gentle light I began to see things the darkness had hidden: the railings of the walkway to the beach, the sea oats on the dunes, the distant horizon, and the gull swooping over the beach in search *By Ruth Graham* of food deposited by the waves. Soon, people walking their dogs emerged from darkened houses.

The sky slowly lightened. Gently. Night gave way to dawn—not to sunshine. I waited. The slowness had forced me to wait and to watch. I began to see color in the sky and grass and water. The day was revealing what the darkness had hidden. The beauty was still there—the dawn revealed it.

If the sun had appeared when I had wanted it to, its light and heat would have been too harsh. I would not have been ready. This way I was able to gently enter the day.

I began to reflect on God's grace, which brings us out of our darkness slowly and gently. How often I get impatient with the darkness. I get impatient with God's leisure. But His way is perfect. As I am still before Him and wait for His timing, I see that it is His graciousness that grants me time to adjust to the new day dawning.

A Prayer for You

Dear Lord, grant me patience and understanding so I may appreciate the perfect timing of your grace that brings me from darkness into light. Amen.

A Prayer for Your Grandchild
FOCUS: Friends

Dear Lord and Father, I pray for my grandchild's social life and his friends. Bring diverse friends into his life who will love and encourage him, who will bring joy and laughter to the good times and comfort and support through difficulties and disappointments. Grant him wisdom and discernment as he selects his friends; help him to avoid cliques that restrict, activities that endanger, and foolish and dangerous behaviors that harm. I ask that you fill his life with close and caring relationships. Amen.

day 70

Come Spring

The desert and the parched land will be glad;
the wilderness will rejoice and blossom.
Like the crocus, it will burst into bloom;
it will rejoice greatly and shout for joy.
—ISAIAH 35:1–2

Grandma Lutrell had a green thumb. She could make anything grow—anywhere and for longer than seemed possible. I loved our walks among her roses. She taught me about the love of God through her gardening.

"Our heavenly Father was the original gardener," she would say. "He planted the first garden in Eden. But Adam didn't tend it too well."

I would giggle.

Oh, how her biblical stories connected with her garden! Once she told me that Jesus was a gardener.

"He is?" I asked in awe.

"Why sure, little Dottie. After He rose again, Mary Magdalene looked at Him and saw Him as a gardener. I believe she saw Him for who He is." She *By Dottie Rambo* would wink and smile as I stood there, thinking of Jesus with a gardening tool instead of a staff.

During Grandma's last winter with us, she called me into her room. The snow fell softly outside her window. She reached for my hand, looked at me for a long time, sighed, and whispered, "Before my roses bloom, I'll be gone to be with Jesus." My eyes filled with tears. "But don't you fret none; I'll be in the best garden with the Gardener. And we'll meet again when He gathers His flowers, come spring."

Whenever I look through a snowy window, I hear the voice of my dear grandmother promising that we'll meet again. I echo her words to my own grandchildren as I tell of the promise of an eternal spring.

A Prayer for You

Lord, I hope in you for all I need to grow and bloom. Give me what I need so I may tend to my grandchildren with the nurturing and watering needed for precious seed in fertile soil. In Jesus's marvelous name, amen.

A Prayer for Your Grandchild
FOCUS: Worship

Dear Lord, you are worthy of worship. Please guide my grandchild to sense the value of worship, especially corporate worship with other believers in the body of Christ. Help her to know the value of meeting together at church with others who share a love for Jesus Christ, and help her to know that worshiping, learning from God's Word, and gaining insights from other believers at church are vital to her spiritual growth.

Blue Hair

"So do not fear, for I am with you;
do not be dismayed, for I am your God.
I will strengthen you and help you;
I will uphold you with my righteous right hand."
—ISAIAH 41:10

When I was diagnosed with stage 4 ovarian cancer and began chemotherapy a few years ago, one of my greatest fears was that my hair loss would frighten my grandchildren. Or maybe I just focused on that immediate fear to cover up lots of other fears I had.

I don't know why hair loss feels so traumatic, but it seems like such a cruel and visible assault in the midst of the many other life changes that cancer brings. So in preparation, I bought a couple of look-just-like-me wigs and one absolutely ridiculous iridescent blue wig for those times I wanted to lighten up *By Carol Kuykendall* and say, "Since we both know I don't have hair, let's have fun with the substitute."

To my surprise and delight, my daughter-in-law bought three-year-old Gabi a similar iridescent blue wig, so we could get used to the idea of wigs by playing dress up together. So there we sat one afternoon, in front of a mirror in my bathroom, putting on our wigs.

"Everyone will think we are so pretty, Oma," Gabi giggled.

"Do you know that Oma is going to wear a wig for a long time?"

"My mommy told me," she nodded. "Can we put on some lipstick too?" she asked, reaching for a tube.

"Good idea . . . Do you know Oma won't have any hair?"

"That's okay, Oma. Can we put on some of this too?" she asked, pointing to some sparkly eye shadow.

Obviously, "no hair" was no problem for Gabi.

Maybe, I thought as I dabbed on some eye shadow, I didn't have to fear those things I thought I feared the most.

A Prayer for You

Lord, children can put our fears into perspective. May I do the same as I keep trusting you with childlike faith.

A Prayer for Your Grandchild
FOCUS: Future Spouse

Dear Lord, if it is your will, I pray my grandchild will be united in a loving and Christian marriage. Keep her sexually pure so she will honor you with her body and mind. As she seeks a spouse who will honor and care for her, give her patience and discernment. May her choice for a life partner be your choice for her, so she and her husband will together glorify you in a lasting love. I pray this in Jesus's name, amen.

day 72

Abundant Blessings

Children are a heritage from the LORD,
offspring a reward from him.
—PSALM 127:3

Seven males had already graced our family (three sons, four grandsons) when the coming of another grandchild was announced. When our middle son, Rick, and his wife came through with a girl, we realized our hoped-for baseball team would now be co-ed. Audrey Lauren Copeland made her entrance into the world on January 23, 2001. Wow! A baby girl! I just stared. Yep. She was a girl all right, with dark curly hair and blue eyes. Adorable? Easily the prettiest, smartest baby in the nursery.

I recall the days when our greatest joy was having Wednesday evenings with Gage (then age eight) and Audrey (then age six). Wednesday nights were memory makers. We began the evening with dinner at the cafeteria: chicken legs, mashed potatoes and white gravy (two servings for Gage), macaroni and cheese, and Jell-O. Then we would go on to church to attend Mission Friends *By Lori Copeland* and Kid's Praise choir. Afterward, we would ask Gage and Audrey what they learned that evening. Sometimes their observations were humorous and other times there were long, dramatic explanations about missionaries and their work. Southern Baptist missionary to China Lottie Moon made a lasting impression on Gage, while cookies usually occupied Audrey's attention.

I can't speak for my grandchildren, but these golden years of Wednesday nights will forever hold a place in my heart and my memory. My first three grandsons were born when I was a young, thirty-nine-year-old grandmother with a child still at home. The last two grandbabies came along when I was more mature, more grandmotherly. Age doesn't matter; it's a grandchild's youthful memories that linger and shape their adult lives.

Grandparenting is a responsibility and a blessing beyond comparison. Leading a child and shaping a child's life can be experienced whether you've been given your own grandchildren or you've been allowed access to other people's children. Memory making costs nothing but a dribble of time and a heaping cupful of love.

A Prayer for You

Dear God, thank you for my grandchildren. I couldn't have known or dreamed of how they would enrich my life and allow me to see the world through innocent eyes. I pray that you use each of these precious lives for your service. As they grow and mature, blind their eyes to evil and transfix their hearts and minds on the eternal. In Jesus's name, amen.

A Prayer for Your Grandchild
FOCUS: School/Career

Dear God, may learning be a joy rather than a chore for my grandchild. May exploration of new ideas bring a sense of wonder, awe, and excitement. Grant him clarity of mind, the ability to concentrate on the task at hand, and recollection of what has been learned. Help him to appreciate the tasks that come easily and to persevere through those that challenge. Amen.

Be Who You Are

The body is not made up of one part but of many . . .
God has placed the parts in the body,
every one of them, just as he wanted them to be.
—1 CORINTHIANS 12:14, 18

Honey, if you are trying to be something you know you aren't, and if you are trying to do things you know you have little ability, patience, passion, commitment, and tolerance for, cut it out!

Be yourself!

The great thing about real authority is that God gives me one thing to do, somebody else another, somebody else something else; or He may give us the same talent but then allow us to exhibit it in different ways. Blending our authority with other people's authority creates the kind of kingdom on earth that personifies God's kingdom in heaven.

The reason Lucifer was kicked out of heaven was that he tried to usurp God's authority and be something he wasn't.

By Thelma Wells

How very stupid when he had the fourth best position in heaven! His jealousy and rebellion cost him his position, his beauty, his ability to make angelic music, and his intimacy with God. When we operate outside of our authority, we experience similar breakdowns.

But that doesn't have to happen to you! Just be who you are, what you are, how you are—the way God made you. It is His grace that creates in you the talents, inclinations, knowledge, and pleasure to be yourself. Grace empowers you to perform the tasks God has given you on earth and to enjoy what He has called you to do.

A Prayer for You

Father, thank you for the gifts and talents you have given me. I confess that so often I'd rather have someone else's! Give me the discernment to recognize the tasks you have given me to do and let go of the rest. Help me to be the unique person you made me to be.

A Prayer for Your Grandchild
FOCUS: Emotional Development

O God, Creator of mind and body, I pray that you will give my grandchild emotional health and strength. Where there is anger, bring peace. Where there is confusion, bring clarity and focus. Where there are dark shadows, cast a ray of hope. Fill her with the sunshine of your Spirit. Warm her with the presence of your peace. In Jesus's name, amen.

day 74

Hats and Hearts

*I will remember the deeds of the LORD;
yes, I will remember your miracles of long ago.*
—PSALM 77:11

"Here are some hats you can play dress up with." I handed seven-year-old Ashley four hats I had been saving for the day hats became popular again, a trend I had finally given up on. "This one was my favorite."

I put on the black felt, one side flipped up Australian style.

Ashley studied me for a moment. "Did people laugh at you when you wore it, Grandmom?"

So much for my sense of fashion.

Later I thought about Ashley's comment and knew it was more than generational tastes that made us view that black felt so differently. The hat held memories for me. I bought it to wear for the dedication of the new dining hall named after my grandfather at the college where he had once been president.

By Gayle Roper

To me the hat stood for Granddad—who had married my then twenty-year-old grandmother when he was forty-two, lived to celebrate their fiftieth wedding anniversary, and worked until he was ninety-three. He had always given me silver dollars and was a whiz at croquet.

How will Ashley remember me? As the woman with weird hats? Undoubtedly. As a grandmother who dearly loved her and the rest of the grands? I pray so.

Memories are such permanent things. Am I giving the grandkids proud, positive ones like my grandfather gave me? Godly ones? Fun ones?

I also want Ashley and the other grandkids to remember God's past care for His people—and for them in particular—so that they will have courage to face life's problems and the challenges that lie ahead.

A Prayer for You

Lord, help me give the grandkids happy and healthy memories that will bulwark them against future hurts, and may they always remember your deeds on their behalf. Amen.

A Prayer for Your Grandchild
FOCUS: Courage

O Father, builder of character and courage, may my grandchild grow strong in the light of your face. Grant him courage to stand for what is right, to guard the truth, and to ensure justice in every aspect of life. May he boldly grow in grace, revere your name, and proudly proclaim you as the Lord of Lords and King of Kings.

day 75

The Light People

*If we walk in the light, as he is in the light,
we have fellowship with one another, and the blood
of Jesus, his Son, purifies us from all sin.*
—1 JOHN 1:7

Do you know any "light people"? Light people spread light wherever they go. Some radiate joy when they enter a room and draw us into that joy. Some stand up for truth when truth comes hard and thus set an example we can follow. Some explain or clarify things that have been difficult to understand. Some have a gentle spirit that penetrates grief, depression, or anxiety and offers compassion and encouragement.

Light people can be very different from one another, but they have two things in common: They all know that Christ brings life and light to the world, and they aren't hung up on their own sins and shortcomings. Instead, they accept God's forgiveness and *By Patricia Sprinkle* get on with spreading light in the world God loves. Another thing about light people: their light—the light of Christ— is contagious across generations.

My father's mother was a light person. She raised nine children on a farm in days when keeping house meant hours of time-consuming work. What her sons remember, though, is that Grandmother always had time to leave her dishpan to join a child in looking at a sunset, or she would abandon the week's washing to help chase a butterfly.

Grandmother died before I was born, but she passed her sense of joy and wonder down to my dad. He passed it to me. Every time I take a child's hand to stand in awe before a hummingbird or enjoy together the miracle of a new flower, I feel very close to her, and I know I am passing on the light.

A Prayer for You

Lord, the One who came to bring light and life to this often dark earth, I want to be a light person. Help me not to just curse the darkness but also to walk in the light. And help me to spread your light to the upcoming generations. Amen.

A Prayer for Your Grandchild
FOCUS: Salvation

Dear Lord, please guide my grandchild to your gift of salvation. I pray that she will come to know you, to love you, and to walk close to you throughout her life. May she boldly claim Jesus as her Lord and Savior. Guide her as she makes choices that have eternal consequences. Help her to follow you each moment of her life. I pray this in Jesus's name, amen.

day 76

A Gracious Tradition

Turn to me and be gracious to me,
for I am lonely and afflicted.
—PSALM 25:16

Each year at Christmastime my family has a number of special traditions. But no tradition is as long-lasting as the day each December when we bake plates of cookies and head to the local retirement home.

Each year, the residents—many of them well into their 80s—look forward with great anticipation to the day when we troop in, ready to entertain them. They come in their Sunday best, many sporting new hairdos and holiday earrings or sweaters. As for us, we bring a ragtag group of babies and teens and friends and family—all of us with red scarves and gloves and Santa hats. A few of the kids can sing well, but for the most part we're a strictly no-talent outfit. The point, we always tell our children, is not the quality of our song, but the quantity of our love.

By Karen Kingsbury

When we sing, I'm always drawn to the women, the grandmothers, the ones who tear up the moment we launch into the first verse of our first song: "Silent Night." It occurs to me anew each time that the nights are all too silent for so many grandmothers. Done with their mothering and even their grandmothering, these women are often lonely and afflicted, the people in their lives too busy for them. As we sing, I look to my own children, and I find myself silently praying that they will be the type of adults who will care about the generations that have come before them.

When we're finished singing, we do the thing we really came to do: We walk through the crowd and give out hugs. And for a brief hour before Christmas, the aging grandmothers in that one place no longer feel lonely and afflicted—because grandmothers desire not only to give love but also to receive it.

A Prayer for You

Dear Lord, help me be mindful of the aging women in my life and community. Let me be part of the solution to their loneliness and affliction, and help me train up my children and grandchildren to love and care for the generations that have come before them. In Christ's name, amen.

A Prayer for Your Grandchild
FOCUS: Character

Dear Lord and Father, I ask that you fill my grandchild with your Spirit so her character reflects your goodness and love. Give her kindness and love for others. Bring joy to her life so she will be a joy to others. Grant her patience and self-control through difficult and trying times. May she show mercy and generosity to those who are less fortunate. Grant her integrity and a sense of justice, and surround her with your peace. Amen.

day 77

A Soup Pot and the Love of a Grandmother

*For the LORD is good;
his steadfast love endures forever.*
—PSALM 100:5 (ESV)

"Grandmothers feed people." These words from my seventeen-year-old grandson made me smile. I am forever offering to make a sandwich, pour a glass of milk, or whip up a batch of his favorite cookies. I skate dangerously close to the stereotypical sitcom grandmother who pursues family members with a plate of cheesy lasagna. Near or far, grandmothers serve their families in many ways. Perhaps acts of service could be called the love language of grandmothers.

For some of us, the time comes when our baking or babysitting days near an end. The grandchildren have entered a new stage of life. So *By Kay Swatkowski* have we. The energy to cook holiday dinners or provide childcare has evaporated. Our resources seem smaller, our limitations larger. Now what?

Corrie ten Boom described how her own mother adapted to this unavoidable time of transition. "Mama's love had always been the kind that acted itself out with a soup pot and sewing basket. But now that these things were taken away, the love seemed as whole as before. She sat in her chair at the window and loved us."

Even when the soup pot is put on the shelf, our love for family is as whole as before. In spite of many changes, a grandmother's love never diminishes. It remains steadfast. What an honor it would be if our visible and unconditional love for our grandchildren pointed them to this enduring truth: "For the LORD is good; his steadfast love endures forever" (Psalm 100:5 ESV).

A Prayer for You

Lord, during times of uncertainty and change, steady me with your love. Help me to display to my grandchildren an unshakable confidence in your steadfast love.

A Prayer for Your Grandchild
FOCUS: God's Love

O God of Love, may my grandchild grasp how wide, high, long and deep is your love for her. May she find comfort in your love.

day 78

Establishing Traditions

Then we your people, the sheep of your pasture,
will praise you forever; from generation
to generation we will proclaim your praise.
—PSALM 79:13

In biblical times families celebrated feasts, holy days, and other special events in festive ways. Today's grandmothers initiate traditions of their own, some hopefully to be passed down to future generations.

For years my husband and I hosted a New Year's "blessing" party for our six grandchildren. Dressed in their Sunday best, they would stand in line waiting for their individual prayer and blessing from their grandparents for the coming year. Then they would eat the goodies I had cooked and laugh at the jokes their cousins told. They loved it!

On the day before each grandchild enters first grade, my friend Rhonda lets him or her pick a restaurant where they can enjoy a scrumptious meal together. Afterward they go shopping for new school clothes. Now the younger ones can't wait until they are old enough to spend the day before they start school with their grandmother.

By Quin Sherrer

Twice a year Mary Jo arms her three granddaughters with cameras and tells them, "Go photograph what God is saying to you as you observe His world." They may hike a mountain, stroll the mall, walk through a park, or even amble around their home. The photos are printed and put in an album. Beside each picture a granddaughter writes what the Lord showed her when she snapped it. "Our photo-journey not only encourages them to hear God but also gives me, their grandmother, great insight into their hearts and lives," Mary Jo said.

Beth has a long-standing tradition that when her grandchildren turn fifteen years old, they may go with her on a short-term mission trip to another country. Today two of them are grown and living overseas as missionaries. Grandmother Beth inspired them both.

The ideas for establishing traditions are endless, and it's never too late to start.

A Prayer for You

Thank you, Lord, for giving me fresh ideas for helping my grandchildren establish new traditions that they may eventually pass on to the next generation. Amen.

A Prayer for Your Grandchild
FOCUS: Relationships at Home

O Lord, I pray that you will bless the home and family of my grandchild. May the relationships she has with her parents and siblings enhance her well-being, support her self-confidence, and increase her faith. May her home life reflect your love, your grace, your compassion, and your peace. Guide her parents to direct her in love and truth, so she will grow into a strong and compassionate individual. Amen.

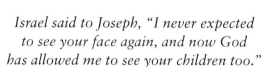

"I Really Miss the Children"

*Israel said to Joseph, "I never expected
to see your face again, and now God
has allowed me to see your children too."*
—GENESIS 48:11

My friend Carolyn and I raised our children at the same time. Recently, we reminisced about those years as we drove together on a short trip. We laughed about the things our boys had done together and mused over the steely will of her daughter, who carved out her place as the boss over three brothers. Having enjoyed our memories, we both fell silent as we rode in the sunlight.

Suddenly, she turned to me and poignantly said, "I really do miss the children." That thought touched a tender place deep within me as I thought, *I really miss the children too.* Our grown children are alive and well, and living close by, but they are all adults now—grown-up people with their own families, jobs, and lives. They are not children anymore, and we miss the children they were.

By Jan Silvious

That's why the gift of grandchildren is so amazing. When Israel (Jacob) and his son Joseph finally had an emotional reunion after so many years of separation, Jacob stated, "Now I am ready to die" (Genesis 46:30). But there remained the additional gift of seeing his grandchildren.

Grandchildren have a way of taking us back to the wonder of having children in the house. Everything that was good about having little ones is suddenly reawakened when that first grandchild is born. Suddenly, a love you never dreamed you could feel for another human being overwhelms you.

When you have grandchildren, everything changes. You take on a new persona. You are given a fresh start. You receive another chance to do it better. The longing you feel for the children who have grown up and left your arms is filled with a little baby who doesn't even know who you are. That's the wonder of being a grandparent. You'll always "miss the children," but somehow when God gives you "grands," He makes it all okay.

A Prayer for You

Father, may I never take the gift of grandchildren for granted. I pray that I will always think to remind them that you love them and that I adore the fact that you made them my grandchildren. Thank you, Lord, for this blessing. Amen.

A Prayer for Your Grandchild
FOCUS: Character

Dear Lord and Father, I ask that you fill my grandchild with your Spirit so her character reflects your goodness and love. Give her kindness and love for others. Bring joy to her life so she will be a joy to others. Grant her patience and self-control through difficult and trying times. May she show mercy and generosity to those who are less fortunate. Grant her integrity and a sense of justice, and surround her with your peace. Amen.

day 80

Leaving a Legacy of Prayer

Let this be written for a future generation,
that a people not yet created may praise the LORD.
—PSALM 102:18

It's true that we as grandmothers desire to leave a godly imprint on future generations. Instead of working hard to leave stock portfolios, heirlooms, money, or property, we can leave them something far more valuable that will last forever; we can leave them a legacy of answered prayer.

Pastor Ron Dunn states: "I can leave my children [grandchildren] an inheritance of answered prayer. I can be confident that long after I'm dead God will be answering the prayers in the lives of my children that I prayed while I was alive. What a privilege and opportunity to leave our children an inheritance like that. To wrap my children up in blankets of intercessory prayer."

By Fern Nichols

I have purposed in my heart to leave that kind of legacy. I have ten grandchildren and pray for each one. It takes time, but in light of eternity, it's worth it. I love praying the will and Word of God in regard to their lives. God's words are powerful and effective when we pray them.

For example, using God's Word I pray that they will

• accept Jesus as their Savior (2 Timothy 3:15),

• please God and desire His plans (Philippians 2:12–13),

- love what God loves and hate what He hates (Psalm 97:10),
- obey their parents (Colossians 3:20),
- be a witness for Christ (Philippians 2:14–16),
- be protected from the evil one (John 17:15), and
- marry a Christian and remain pure until marriage (2 Corinthians 6:14).

Purpose in your heart to be a praying grandmother. We can do a lot of wonderful things for our grandchildren, but their lives are truly transformed when we pray.

A Prayer for You

Eternal God, I purpose in my heart to pray daily for my grandchildren. May I leave a legacy in the lives of my grandkids that will change the course of history. Encourage my heart to know that when I pray, I trust your mighty hand to work out your will in their lives. In Jesus's name, amen.

A Prayer for Your Grandchild
FOCUS: Prayer

Gracious Father, thank you for the avenue of prayer. Holy Spirit, please instill within the heart of my grandchild the desire to talk with you in prayer—to be open and transparent with you and to trust you enough to share his cares, prayers, and concerns. Amen.

day 81

Grandma Sally's Prayers

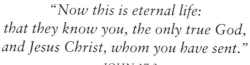

"Now this is eternal life:
that they know you, the only true God,
and Jesus Christ, whom you have sent."
—JOHN 17:3

As grandmothers, we have a special place in our hearts and thoughts for our grandchildren. We can share our knowledge and faith with them and use our influence to steer them in the ways of the Lord.

But most important, we grandmas can pray for our grandchildren to receive Christ as Savior. Then we can pray that we—or someone else—will have the opportunity to share the simple gospel with them. And finally, we can pray that they in turn will be used by God to influence others.

After the funeral for her ninety-six-year-old grandmother, Jennie and her family gathered at the old homestead to celebrate her life. They sang some of her favorite hymns. Then they listened to a cassette tape Grandma Sally had made in an effort to pass down to her descendants some of her homespun wisdom and poetry and a short account of her spiritual journey.

By Quin Sherrer

Jennie later told me, "I suddenly realized I am a Christian because of Grandma's prayers. She lived so far from our family that I didn't see her often, but whenever I was about to end a visit, she would say a short prayer over me. When I heard her voice on the tape, I knew for certain her prayers had followed me all my life."

Grandma Sally's example shows us that regardless of distance, our prayers can affect and reach our grandchildren. Not only can we find ways to tell them about Jesus but we also can pray that others will encourage them in their Christian faith.

A Prayer for You

Lord, I pray that my grandchildren will come to know Jesus at an early age. Show me what to say to my grandchildren—in a letter, a phone call, or a face-to-face conversation—that will encourage them to love you always and trust you with their lives. Amen.

A Prayer for Your Grandchild
FOCUS: Salvation

Dear Lord, please guide my grandchild to your gift of salvation. I pray that she will come to know you, to love you, and to walk close to you throughout her life. May she boldly claim Jesus as her Lord and Savior. Guide her as she makes choices that have eternal consequences. Help her to follow you each moment of her life. I pray this in Jesus's name, amen.

day 82

Invest Your Influence

"His master replied, 'Well done, good and faithful
servant! You have been faithful with a few things;
I will put you in charge of many things.
Come and share your master's happiness!'"
—MATTHEW 25:23

You are a person of influence. You have the power to influence others. What are you doing with your power to influence?

It's tough to fully realize the power of our influence. Some days we spend our time in hidden service—babysitting a grandchild, running errands, helping out with the daily busyness of life. During those times we may wonder about our "return on investment." Who really cares? Did anyone notice? Other moments in our days and weeks are more convincing of their significance—presenting a report, chairing a committee, praying with a gravely ill friend. During those times we know that we are needed and that what we are giving will bring results.

By Elisa Morgan

Matthew 25:14–30 presents the parable of the talents. In this familiar story, we read of the faithful servants who invested all they had been given, increased their possessions, and pleased their master to the point that they received more to continue investing. And we read of the fearful servant who plunked the goods down in a hole, hoping to just hold on to them until they were once again required.

We tend to "rate" the value of what we've been given just as much as we rate what we do with it. Bring a measurable return. Small, seemingly ordinary abilities may be overlooked. In truth, God gives vital capacities to each of us. Our job is to wake up to His giftings—fully and wholly—and invest them. Our money, yes. Our faith, of course. But especially our influence over those in our lives.

A Prayer for You

Dear Master, who has entrusted influence to each of us, I pray that you would reorient my perspective to see the sacred capacity that is much needed from me in your kingdom work: my influence. I freely offer it to my children and grandchildren and to those I work and serve alongside, yielding responsibility for the results of this investment to you. Amen.

A Prayer for Your Grandchild
FOCUS: Talents

Dear Lord, the giver of gifts, bless my grandchild as he develops his talents. Help him identify his talents and be proud and confident of the gifts you have given him. Give him patience and understanding, Lord, so he will not grow weary of striving and searching to reach the goals you have set for him. May each milestone bring satisfaction and a healthy desire for greater achievement and success to bring glory to you. Amen.

day 83

God Is Faithful

*"God is not human, that he should lie,
not a human being, that he should change
his mind. Does he speak and then not act?
Does he promise and not fulfill?"*
—NUMBERS 23:19

I took a deep breath and composed myself. The hospital door rolled open, and I saw my daughter, Lisa, inside. Our eyes met and locked. I hoped she wouldn't notice my legs shaking beneath my coat.

"The doctor thinks Alexia has a tumor in her leg." Her words seemed surreal; fear clutched my throat.

"When will we know?" I tried to sound calm, but the tears in my eyes betrayed me.

"Not soon enough," she whispered.

When faced with difficulties, I have always clung to the promise that God walks with me through every trial. In each circumstance, God has proven that He can be trusted and that He is 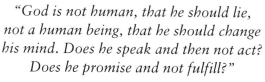 faithful to bring me though every storm.

By Dawn Scott Damon

But would God's grace be enough this time? In spite of His continual faithfulness, I wavered.

It can happen in a moment. That unexpected call—a tragedy or sudden storm that rocks our world and shakes us to the core. God allows a test to come into our life, and we wonder if we can endure it. But God's Word is true. His grace is sufficient! His love is enough! His arm is strong enough to sustain us and lift us up. When we reach for Him, we will find His grace reaching back. God promises that His strong arm will uphold us, and He always fulfills His promises.

We hugged with tears of joy as the doctor informed us that my granddaughter was perfect—no tumors.

I finally exhaled, "Thank you, Jesus."

A Prayer for You

Heavenly Father, you are strong and mighty to save. I trust your ability to sustain me in all of life's circumstances. I turn my eyes upon you and believe that you will enable me to endure and that you will be with me through every storm. Amen.

A Prayer for Your Grandchild
FOCUS: Physical Well-Being

Almighty God, Creator of us all, I pray that you will watch over my grandchild's physical development. May he grow in strength through the stages of his life. As he grows in awareness of his body, help him to understand that each body develops uniquely yet is within your plan and your control. Please guard his health so his diseases are few, his injuries are minor, and his infirmities are brief. Amen.

day 84

Teach the Children

*These commandments that I give you today are
to be on your hearts. Impress them on your children.
Talk about them when you sit at home
and when you walk along the road,
when you lie down and when you get up.*
—DEUTERONOMY 6:6–7

One evening when my grandchildren Joshua and Mimi (Jessica) came over, God gave me an idea of how to teach them the Bible story of blind Bartimaeus receiving his sight (see Mark 10:46–52; Luke 18:35–43). I decided to turn it into a little play. I shared the story from the Bible and had them practice their lines.

By Fern Nichols

The drama went something like this: I was the friend who led Mimi (Bartimaeus) to Jesus. Joshua was Jesus, sitting on the couch. I led Mimi around the house with her little eyes squinted. I brought her to Jesus.

Joshua: "What do you want me to do for you?"

Mimi: "I want to see."

Joshua touched her eyes and said, "See."

Mimi opened her eyes very wide and shouted and jumped up and down saying, "I can see! I can see!" Then I danced with her all around the living room. We played Bartimaeus many times that evening, with the kids exchanging roles. That night the Word came alive to them. Jesus came alive.

I try to live out Deuteronomy 6:6–7 by being observant in everyday happenings and relating them to God. One time we played outside and saw a lizard scamper across the sidewalk. We talked about who made the lizard and how awesome God, the creator, is. And of course that led to a discussion about other insects and creatures.

Yes, sometimes I get tired, but the joy of influencing my grandchildren for Jesus when we sit at home, when we walk along the road, when we lie down, and when we get up is a great gift from the Lord. I desire to impress upon their hearts that there is a God who loves them and desires a relationship with them. There is no greater gift than to love my children's children to Jesus.

A Prayer for You

Sovereign Lord of heaven and earth, I pray that by your grace you would place on my heart an excitement to live out this passage from Deuteronomy. Give me wisdom in how to do it in my daily activities and in special times together with my grandchildren. Help me to be especially creative with the grandchildren I don't see often. May I know that my godly influence can change the lives of my grandchildren. In Jesus's name, amen.

A Prayer for Your Grandchild
FOCUS: Creativity

Lord, you are the master of creativity. You wove this universe into its beautiful existence with just a word, and when you did, you splashed spectacular wonder throughout. But even more, you allowed us to contribute to the beauty of the world with the skills you gave us to create new and lovely things. Guide my grandchild to embrace his creativity and to use it for your praise.

Caring for Each One

*"Suppose one of you has a hundred sheep
and loses one of them. Doesn't he leave
the ninety-nine in the open country
and go after the lost sheep until he finds it?"*
—LUKE 15:4

I never really knew my grandmothers. Grandma Doris on my mom's side died months before I was born, and Grandma Rosemary on my dad's side died when I was just three. Maybe for that reason I was drawn to my husband's Grandma Polly.

Grandma Polly was a farm girl in her day, tall and strong and able to keep up with the best of the boys. She raised seven kids, and none of them even considered talking back to her or letting her down. By the time I met her, Grandma Polly was in her mid–70s, but she hadn't lost a step. Not only could she keep *By Karen Kingsbury* her great-grandchildren—my kids—in line but also her mind was as sharp as it had ever been.

In a short time I came to see Grandma Polly as the grandmother I never had, the one I always wanted when I was a young girl. Her role in my life reminded me of the picture that all of us are like sheep, wandering and confused, without a whole lot of sense until we come under the care of the Good Shepherd. Though Grandma Polly had many children and dozens of grandchildren and great-grandchildren, she made me feel like I was the only granddaughter in her life.

That's the way it is with Jesus. He'll go after the one sheep and leave for a while the ninety-nine, just to show how much He loves us. Grandma Polly loved me and gave me extra attention, and she helped me see her faith and love for Christ at work. She died when our daughter was ten. I'm not sure Grandma Polly ever knew how much her kindness meant to me, but I know her presence in my life was a gift from God.

A Prayer for You

Dear Lord, help me to look for the lost and lonely in my life, especially as my children have kids of their own. A young person might not be my own child or grandchild, but help me to reach out to that one, the way you, the Good Shepherd, reach out to me. Amen.

A Prayer for Your Grandchild
FOCUS: Self-Image

O loving God, I praise you for creating my grandchild as a special, unique individual. Now I ask you to help her appreciate her uniqueness. Build up her self-image so she can enjoy her individuality. Help her to stand for who she is, where she has come from, and what she believes in. Encourage her not only to have hopes and dreams for the future but also to enjoy each day as it comes. In Jesus's name, amen.

Let Your Light Shine!

"You are the light of the world . . .
Let your light shine before others,
that they may see your good deeds
and glorify your Father in heaven."
—MATTHEW 5:14, 16

My grandmother was born in 1894, married at age four-teen, and raised thirteen children. She had a third-grade education, but I have always thought her to be one of the wisest women I have ever known. She never wore makeup, but to me she was beautiful. Although we did not see each other often, I loved her deeply.

As I think about her life, I recall her welcoming embrace, her broad smile, and her gravelly voice saying, "Get in this house!" Her weathered face showed the years she spent hoeing in her garden. She once said, "If a storm was coming, and I had to choose to go to a storm cellar or the pea patch, I'd choose the pea patch because it has saved my life so many times."

I remember her as soft, kind, and at peace. Every time I was with her, she was always the same—loving, accepting of her circumstances, and wanting to serve any and all who came into her home. She had an *By Cynthia Heald* amazing ability to make each person feel special. I am one of thirty-five grandchildren, and we all agree that each of us felt we were her favorite.

Her good deeds consisted of loving unconditionally, being a role model of what it looks like to trust God, and sharing anything she had to help others. Her faithful serving is still remembered and continues to result in praise to our Father in heaven.

A few years before her death, I was visiting with her, and she told me that her favorite song was "This Little Light of Mine." The lyrics go, "This little light of mine, I'm going let it shine." And so she did.

A Prayer for You

Father, thank you for godly grandmothers who love you and are willing to let their light shine in this dark world. As I reflect on the godly women who have shaped my life, I pray that my life, like theirs, will result in praise and glory to your name. Amen.

A Prayer for Your Grandchild
FOCUS: Emotional Development

O God, Creator of mind and body, I pray that you will give my grandchild emotional health and strength. Where there is anger, bring peace. Where there is confusion, bring clarity and focus. Where there are dark shadows, cast a ray of hope. Fill her with the sunshine of your Spirit. Warm her with the presence of your peace. In Jesus's name, amen.

A Marriage Like Grandma's

*Therefore shall a man leave his father
and his mother, and shall cleave unto his wife:
and they shall be one flesh.*
—GENESIS 2:24 (KJV)

In the beginning God created marriage, and it—along with all God had made—was "very good" (Genesis 1:31). Intended as the closest and most satisfying of all human relationships, the marriage bond remains strong when we follow the three principles in this passage: leaving, "cleaving," and becoming one. It doesn't matter if we have been married for five months or fifty years, these three principles are foundational for building a strong, *By Claudia Arp* healthy, and loving Christian marriage. It's this model of marriage that I pray we will pass on to future generations. Grandchildren are blessed when they are able to observe a "very good" marriage.

Look at your marriage and see if you are living out these three principles. "Leaving" our parents many years ago was the easy part, but that's not all we need to leave. Over the years, leaving involves realigning our priorities from what I want for *me* to what I want for *us*. It includes staying in the relationship through hard times, being faithful, and putting our marriage first. Being *united* (the word some translations use instead of to *cleave*) involves being best friends and soul mates—making choices that pull us together rather than those that put distance between us. Becoming "one flesh" means that we are lovers for life. God created the sexual relationship, and He is the one who placed the passion deep within our hearts to love each other physically.

Think about your own marriage as a model for your children and grandchildren. What might you need to "leave" to make your relationship a higher priority? What steps do you need to take to become better friends and soul mates? And how's your love life? Do your grandchildren see you display a tender, playful, and loving attitude? Do your grandchildren look at you and say, "I want to have a marriage like my grandparents have"? They will if you live out Genesis 2:24.

A Prayer for You

Dear Father, thank you that in the beginning you created marriage and that you can empower me to leave behind a me-centered attitude, unite with my husband, and be one with him. Thank you that my husband and I can be a positive marriage model for our grandchildren. Amen.

A Prayer for Your Grandchild
FOCUS: Future Spouse

Dear Lord, if it is your will, I pray my grandchild will be united in a loving and Christian marriage. Keep her sexually pure so she will honor you with her body and mind. As she seeks a spouse who will honor and care for her, give her patience and discernment. May her choice for a life partner be your choice for her, so she and her husband will together glorify you in a lasting love. I pray this in Jesus's name, amen.

day 88

My Turn

I am reminded of your sincere faith, which first lived
in your grandmother Lois and in your mother Eunice
and, I am persuaded, now lives in you also.
—2 TIMOTHY 1:5

My dad died when I was an infant, and my widowed grandmother came to live with us so my mom could work. I have lots of memories of Grandma—she was a wonderful storyteller and could entertain children and adults alike for hours. But the predominant memory I have of Grandma is of her sitting in the chair near the fireplace with her big, black, and very worn Bible open on her lap. She read it, she knew it, and she lived it.

By Robin Lee Hatcher

I was too young to realize the importance of Grandma's example to me—she passed away when I was twelve—but as an adult, I've looked back often in thanksgiving for the witness of her faith as well as the witness of my mother's faith.

Now it's my turn to be an example to my grandchildren. I want them to see me living my faith daily, to see my hunger for God's Word, His touch, and His voice. I pray that years from now when they look back and think of me, they will remember the relationship I had with God and be thankful for it. I pray that the legacy of my grandmother's faith will be passed from generation to generation until Christ returns.

A Prayer for You

Abba, Father, help me to be a godly example to those I love, especially to those in my family. Thank you for the blessing of children and grandchildren. May each of them and their entire households come to believe in the Lord Jesus. To you, God, be the glory. Amen.

A Prayer for Your Grandchild
FOCUS: Protection from Worldliness

O Sovereign Lord, the world surrounds my grandchild, pressing in and tempting him in so many ways. Help him set appropriate limits. Give him sound judgment to choose wisely. Guard him from temptation; protect him from physical and mental predators; lead him into paths of righteousness and light. And reassure me with your promise that you are holding him in your hands. Amen.

day 89

Pass It On

Tell it to your children,
and let your children tell it to their children,
and their children to the next generation.
—JOEL 1:3

The Israelites had a long history of passing on to subsequent generations their stories of God's wonderful acts of deliverance and provision (see Exodus 10:1–2; 12:23–27; Deuteronomy 4:9; Psalm 78:1–6). But in his book, the prophet Joel exhorted the people to tell future generations about a devastating invasion of locusts. Confronted by this crisis, he called on young and old alike to repent and return to the Lord. Joel called for change and renewal in his generation—renewal that would perpetuate through future generations.

The older I get, the more I realize how important it is to pass the torch along to my children and grandchildren. After my mother died, I was sorting through her things and found a small devotional journal in which my grandmother had recorded her devotions

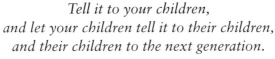

By Claudia Arp and prayers. My mother had been given this journal and had received comfort from it for years. Now I can pass it on to my own children and grandchildren.

Why not pass on your own "story"? Think about how meaningful it might be for your great-grandchildren to someday read about your spiritual journey, your experience of God's grace as well as His loving discipline. If you don't especially like to write, you could record history in other ways, such as by making photo albums or videotaping a message to future generations in your family. Talk about the highlights of your life and how God has walked with you through the days and years—both the mountaintops *and* the valleys. Someday it may be a legacy that your descendants will appreciate.

A Prayer for You

Dear Lord, please help me to pass on a godly heritage to my children and grandchildren. Give me opportunities to talk about you and tell my grandchildren stories of how you have worked in my life.

A Prayer for Your Grandchild
FOCUS: Emotional Development

O God, Creator of mind and body, I pray that you will give my grandchild emotional health and strength. Where there is anger, bring peace. Where there is confusion, bring clarity and focus. Where there are dark shadows, cast a ray of hope. Fill her with the sunshine of your Spirit. Warm her with the presence of your peace. In Jesus's name, amen.

Leaving a Legacy

After that whole generation had been gathered
to their ancestors, another generation
grew up who knew neither the LORD
nor what he had done for Israel.
—JUDGES 2:10

What an incredible denunciation! The mothers and fathers and grandmothers and grandfathers in Israel had been completely lax in their responsibility to teach their children (see God's command in Deuteronomy 6:4–7). If children of any generation grow up in an atmosphere void of instruction about God and His actions, the only ones to blame are the parents and grandparents. I take this verse very seriously. I hope we all do! I want to leave something more than my china or silver

By Jean E. Syswerda

or a car to my grandchildren. I want to leave a legacy of a grandmother who was a woman of faith.

A legacy can be many things. It can be the product of wise spending and investment . . . money left behind for children and grandchildren. It can be a love for a skill or an athletic ability. It can be an aptitude for certain skills. It can be a sunny disposition or a grumpy temperament. It can be a house brimming with laughter or a house filled with harsh words. It can be the heritage of faithful living that you build around your children and grandchildren.

As grandmothers we have the grand opportunity of doing now what we might think we didn't do so well the first time around. Our grandchildren present us with an amazing second chance. Let's not take that opportunity lightly. We have the chance to ensure that their generation doesn't grow up knowing nothing of God or His deeds. We can let everything the years have taught us about God spill over in abundance into their lives, building a legacy of faith and trust, and creating an inheritance of knowing all about God's goodness and depending on Him.

A Prayer for You

Dear Lord, as I spend time with my grandchildren, help me to live a life in front of them that teaches them about you. May my words and actions reveal my love of you. May I take every teachable moment and use it fully to bring my grandchildren the truth of your love for them. Thank you, Lord, for loving all of us with an amazing and a saving love. Amen.

A Prayer for Your Grandchild
FOCUS: Relationships at Home

O Lord, I pray that you will bless the home and family of my grandchild. May the relationships she has with her parents and siblings enhance her well-being, support her self-confidence, and increase her faith. May her home life reflect your love, your grace, your compassion, and your peace. Guide her parents to direct her in love and truth, so she will grow into a strong and compassionate individual. Amen.

Get to Know the Writers

Claudia Arp is a marriage and family educator, speaker, and coauthor (with husband David) of many books, including *The Second Half of Marriage, Empty Nesting,* and the *10 Great Dates* series. They are the founders of Marriage Alive International, Inc., which is dedicated to building better marriages and families. Their website can be found at 10greatdates .org. The Arps, who live in Northern Virginia, have three sons and eight grandchildren.

Sheila Bailey has developed a ministry as a Bible teacher and conference speaker, which has garnered for her an honorary doctorate from Dallas Baptist University. Sheila has spoken at numerous events across the country, including the Our Daily Bread Ministries One-Day Bible Conference in 2017. Her outreach, Sheila B. Ministries, can be accessed at sheilab.org. She and her late husband, Dr. E. K. Bailey, have two daughters and two granddaughters.

Cheryl Baker and her husband, John, were cofounders of a Christ-based recovery program, Celebrate Recovery, at Saddleback Church in California. Cheryl worked for twenty years as the director of a preschool, and now she travels nationwide helping to train churches in the Celebrate Recovery curriculum. Cheryl and John have two children and five grandchildren.

Emilie Barnes (1938–2016) and her husband, Bob, were married more than sixty years. Emilie taught women creative ways to get organized through her bestselling books and her successful ministry More Hours in My Day. Among her books are *More Hours in My Day*, *If Teacups Could Talk*, and *15 Minutes Alone with God*. She and Bob had two children, five grandchildren, and three great grandchildren. Emilie went home to heaven on August 31, 2016, after a long battle with cancer.

Natalie J. Block and her husband Greg live near Cadillac, Michigan, where Natalie is a freelance editor and writer. She has assisted in various Bible study projects, including the *Zondervan Study Bible*, *Entering God's Presence* study on prayer, and the *NIV Study Bible*. She and Greg direct their church's prayer ministry.

Dee Brestin is known for the Dee Brestin Bible Study series and her books such as *The Friendships of Women* and *Idol Lies*. When her husband, Steve, was fifty-nine years old, he died of cancer. Together, she and Steve had five children and fourteen grandchildren. In the summer of 2010, three daughters and one daughter-in-law each gave birth to a girl. Dee lives in Door County, Wisconsin, where she is involved in the growth of a new church plant called The Orchard. You can find out more about Dee at deebrestin.com

Lori Copeland is a prolific writer of Christian fiction, including *Amelia and the Captain,* which is Book 3 of the Sisters of Mercy Flats series. A complete list of Lori's books can be found at loricopeland.com. Her book *Stranded in Paradise* premiered as a Hallmark Channel Original Movie in 2014. In 2000 she was inducted into the Missouri Writers Hall of Fame. Lance and Lori live in Springfield, Missouri, and are the proud parents of three, grandparents of six, and great-grandparents of two.

Carol Cymbala directs the 280-voice Brooklyn Tabernacle Choir in Brooklyn, New York. This choir has won multiple Grammy Awards and has sung at Radio City Music Hall, Madison Square Garden, and Carnegie Hall. Her husband, Jim, is the pastor of the Brooklyn Tabernacle. Carol and Jim have three children and seven grandchildren.

Dawn Scott Damon uses a variety of avenues to share Christ's love with others. As co-pastor of Tribes Church in suburban Grand Rapids, Michigan, she provides vision for the people who worship with her. As an author, she has written *When a Woman You Love Was Abused.* As a blogger, she helps women with her Freedom Girl Sisterhood blog. She and her husband Paul enjoy the company of five children and nine grandchildren.

Ruth A. DeJager is a freelance editor who lives in Marne, Michigan, with her husband Rick. Some of her editing projects over the years include the *NIV*

Women's Devotional Bible and the *NIV Collegiate Bible*. While working as an editor at Zondervan, she assisted such notable writers as Joni Eareckson Tada, Philip Yancey, and President Jimmy Carter.

Ruth Graham is known for speaking and writing about the difficulties she has faced in life. Her book *In Every Pew Sits a Broken Heart* addresses how hard life can be and the help God brings in tough times. She also wrote *Step into the Bible*, a book of family devotionals. Ruth has three children and nine grandchildren.

Helen Haidle has written or cowritten more than fifty books for children. Among those books are *What Would Jesus Do?*, *The Creation Story for Children*, and *Journey to the Cross*. Her first book *He Is My Shepherd*, illustrated by her husband, David, won a C. S. Lewis Silver Award.

Robin Lee Hatcher is an award-winning writer of novels. Among her awards is the Romance Writers of America Lifetime Achievement Award, which she received in 2001. Her *Patterns of Love* won a RITA Award for best inspirational romance of 1999. She lives in Idaho and has two daughters and six grandchildren.

Cynthia Heald, who has four children and twelve grandchildren, has worked side-by-side with her husband, Jack, with The Navigators since 1978. Together, they have produced a series of Bible studies on marriage. She also wrote a study called *Becoming a*

Woman of Excellence, which has been in print for more than thirty years.

Donna Huisjen is a veteran Bible editor who has also written extensively. Among her books are *My Tall Book of Psalms, Every Single Day: Devotional Moments for the Solo Mom*, and *A Bible Lover Reflects on the Psalms*. As an editor, she worked on the award-winning *NIV Archaeological Bible*, produced by Zondervan. Donna has three daughters and one granddaughter.

Neta Jackson has teamed up with her husband, Dave, to write more than 120 books. Their most popular series was the Trailblazer books, which told the stories of great Christian heroes for kids. They have also written *Heroes in Black History*. The Evanston, Illinois, couple has three children and several grandchildren.

Carol Kent is the bestselling author of *When I Lay My Isaac Down*. Her popular Speak Up conference equips speakers and writers in their craft. She and her husband, Gene, also founded an organization called Speak Up for Hope, which seeks to help families of inmates. A noted public speaker, Carol appears internationally to provide help and hope to her audiences.

Karen Kingsbury is a sportswriter-turned-novelist who has some impressive stats: More than fifty novels—with twenty-five million books in print, at least twelve bestsellers, and numerous movies being produced based on her books. Don and Karen Kingsbury have five sons, one daughter, and one grandson.

Carol Kuykendall survived cancer and now relishes being a grandmother (or Oma) to ten grandchildren. She and her husband Lynn live in Boulder, Colorado, where she has a ministry to women called Stories—a unique community where women share what is going on in their lives. Carol has written several books, including *Real Moms* and *What Every Mom Needs*.

Florence Littauer's life work was honored when she was named on one list of "100 Christian Women Who Changed the Twentieth Century." Among her many books is *Personality Plus* and several follow-up books on the subject of personality. She has also been known as a popular public speaker for many years. She and her husband Fred (who died in 2002) had two daughters, one son, and five grandchildren.

Michelle R. Loyd-Paige has an earned doctorate in sociology from Purdue University and is the executive director to the president for diversity and inclusion at Calvin College in Grand Rapids, Michigan. Among her writing credits is the coauthorship of *Set Us Free: What the Church Needs to Know from Survivors of Abuse.* Her husband, Darrell, was mayor of Muskegon Heights, Michigan, for twenty-five years.

Rebecca Lutzer, a registered nurse, has long sought to help women serve God faithfully. This led to a book she co-wrote with her husband, Erwin, the pastor emeritus of Moody Church in Chicago. The book, *Jesus, Lover of a Woman's Soul*, showed how Jesus changed everything for women with His compassion for them. The Lutzers have three daughters and eight grandchildren.

Karen Mains directs the ministry Hungry Souls (hungry souls.org), where it is her goal to help people who are hungry to know God better. Over the years, Karen has written a number of books, including *Open Hearts, Open Homes*; *Tales of the Resistance*; and *Comforting One Another*. She and her husband David have four children and seven grandchildren.

Victoria McAfee set aside her middle-school dream of becoming a writer to pursue what her family called "a real job." After studying psychology, she began her career working in an orphanage in Illinois. But with her love of Christ and her training, she later began to write while waiting for the birth of her first child. Among her publications are *Restoring Broken Vessels*, *Children and Sexual Abuse*, and *In-depth Bible Study for Sisters*—all through InterVarsity Press. Victoria has three children and one grandchild and lives with her husband in Milwaukee.

Elisa Morgan is one of the voices of *Discover the Word*, the daily radio broadcast of Our Daily Bread Ministries. In addition, Elisa has written several books, including the *Mom's Devotional Bible*, *She Did What She Could*, and *Hello, Beauty Full*. Elisa and her husband Evan have two children and two grandchildren. After being the CEO of MOPS International for many years, she is now the President Emerita of MOPS.

Fern Nichols is the founder of Mothers in Prayer International, an organization that has encouraged young mothers for years. She has penned a number of books on prayer: *Moms in Prayer, Mom's Little Book of Powerful Prayers*, and *Moms in Touch*. She and her husband Rle have four children and ten grandchildren.

Margaret Fishback Powers spent more than forty years in education teaching music. She and her husband, Paul, started a ministry called Little People's Ministry Association to help reach kids with the gospel. She also wrote a book called *A Heart for Children* to inspire kids and parents alike. She is the mother of two daughters and the grandmother of four.

Dottie Rambo (1934–2008), well known for her Grammy- and Dove Award-winning career in music, died in a tour bus accident in Missouri. She was traveling from a concert in Illinois to a scheduled event in Texas when the bus ran off an interstate highway and crashed. Among the most famous of the songs Dottie wrote in her illustrious career is "We Shall Behold Him." But to her grandchildren, she will always be remembered as GranDot.

Patricia Raybon worked for many years as a journalist for *The Denver Post* and other publications before becoming a journalism professor at the University of Colorado, Boulder. Now writing full-time, she has penned a number of books, including *My First White Friend* and *I Told the Mountain to Move*, a prayer memoir. She and her husband Dan have two daughters and five grandchildren.

Diane Proctor Reeder is a Detroit-based author, editor, and playwright who has worked with numerous Christian authors, motivational speakers, and artists. Her plays focus on the powerful women whose stories are merely hinted at in the Bible. Her book *What the Word BE: Why Black English is the King's (James) English* is available on Amazon. You can find Diane at www.dianereeder.com.

Debby Kerner Rettino and her husband Ernie will be remembered by a generation of kids as the creators of Psalty the Singing Psalm Book, which was hugely popular among children in the 1980s and 90s—and is still being used today. Debbie earned a Doctor of Ministry degree a few years ago. She served as director of worship at Saddleback Church for many years. The Rettinos have two daughters and four grandchildren.

Doris Wynbeek Rikkers was the executive editor of *The Grandmother's Bible*, from which this book was taken. She has been in publishing for over forty years, with Bible projects as her passion and specialty. For seventeen years, she developed and edited all NIV Bibles released by Zondervan. She now leads her own business as consultant, writer, and editor, and has also written numerous children's books. Doris lives in West Michigan and loves to garden, read, cook, travel, and sit on the beach. She also enjoys spending time with friends and family, especially her grandchildren.

Gayle Roper is an award-winning author of contemporary mysteries. She has written more than forty books including fiction books *A Stranger's Wish* and *A Secret Identity*, plus the nonfiction *A Widow's Journey*. Her husband, Chuck, a pastor, died in 2010. Gayle has two sons and five grandchildren.

Quin Sherrer has a passion for teaching Christians to pray. That has led her to write a number of books on the subject, including *How to Pray for Your Children*, *Miracles Happen When You Pray*, and *A Mother's Guide to Praying for Your Children*. During her award-winning career, Quin has written twenty-nine books. She and her husband LeRoy have six grandchildren.

Jan Silvious is not only a renowned writer for books such as *Big Girls Don't Whine* and *Foolproofing Your Life* but she is also a sought-after speaker. She has appeared at Women of Faith events nationwide, at Moody's Founders Week, and on the radio co-hosting with Kay Arthur the program *Precept Live*. She and her husband, Charlie, have three children and five grandchildren.

Patricia Sprinkle knew she wanted to be a writer when was a high school freshman. And after college, she moved by herself to Scotland to begin her career. These many years later, she has more than thirty books to her credit. She has written mysteries (*Who Left That Body in the Rain*, for example), and nonfiction (*Women Who Do Too Much* and *Children Who Do Too Little*). Patricia's husband, Bob, died in 2014; they had been married forty-three years. She has two children and three grandchildren.

Kay Swatkowski is a pastoral counselor, speaker, and writer. She focuses her passion on a variety of issues related to families and spiritual direction. Kay has written two books: *A Grandmother's Prayers* and *Make Yourself at Home*. She coauthored the second book with her husband, Ray, a pastor who planted several churches in the United States. Together, they served three years as missionaries in France. Kay and Ray have four children and seven grandchildren.

Jean E. Syswerda helped develop many best-selling Bibles as an editor at Zondervan, including the *NIV Women's Devotional Bible*. She has coauthored such popular books as *Women of the Bible* and the *Read with Me Bible*. She and her husband John have three children and eight grandchildren.

Jeannette Taylor has worked in the Bible publishing industry more than thirty years and was instrumental in developing many best-selling titles, including *The Grandmother's Bible*, from which this book is derived. She has worked for Zondervan and also started two companies, JET Marketing and Somersault. Jeannette lives in West Michigan with her family and enjoys being an adjunct professor, serving her church, and spending time outdoors.

Thelma Wells, a sought-after speaker, likes to "Tell everyone how they can BEE their best in Christ." She has appeared on many TV programs including *Dr. Phil*, the *700 Club*, and *Life Today*. "Mama T," as she is sometimes called, has spoken in person to more than a million people during her lifetime of motivating and inspiring others.

Bobbie Wolgemuth (1950–2014) died of cancer in November 2014 having served the Christian community through her writing for decades. Among her books were *God's Wisdom for a Mother's Heart*, *With Love from Mom*, and *Hymns for a Kid's Heart*, which she coauthored with Joni Eareckson Tada. Bobbie and her husband Robert had two daughters and five grandchildren.

Scripture Index

OLD TESTAMENT

NEW TESTAMENT

Help us get the word out!

Our Daily Bread Publishing exists to feed the soul with the Word of God.

If you appreciated this book, please let others know.

- Pick up another copy to give as a gift.
- Share a link to the book or mention it on social media.
- Write a review on your blog, on a bookseller's website, or at our own site (ourdailybreadpublishing.org).
- Recommend this book for your church, book club, or small group.

Connect with us:

f @ourdailybread

⟲ @ourdailybread

𝕐 @ourdailybread

Our Daily Bread Publishing
PO Box 3566
Grand Rapids, Michigan 49501 USA

✉ books@odb.org